Quick & Easy
Soups

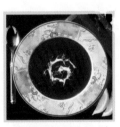

p

Contents

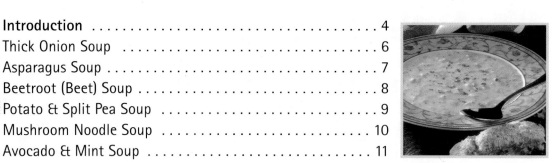

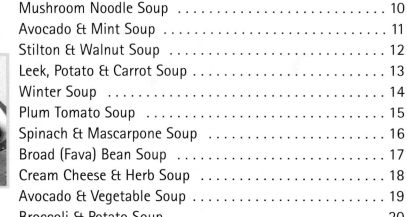

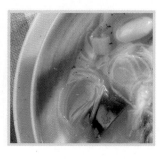

Introduction

The traditional way to start a meal is with a soup, but soups can also provide satisfying meals by themselves making them ideal for lunches, starters, and main courses. They are quick and easy to prepare, provide a filling, healthy meal and can be made from an almost infinite number of ingredients. From the most traditional of Tomato Soups to Chinese Wonton Soup, Italian Minestrone or a wholesome vegetable winter-warmer, you are sure to find a soup to suit any occasion. These recipes suggest dishes that are quick and simple to prepare but which will provide a healthy, tasty dish for you, your family and your guests.

Stock

For the best results use home-made stock as the base for your soup. Use the liquor left from cooking vegetables and the juices from fish and meat to make the best stock; this way your soup will be rich in vitamins and nutrients from the cooked food — and remember it can easily be frozen in small amounts and used the next time you are making soup. Ready-made stock cubes are an alternative to fresh stock if you are short of time, but be careful as the strong flavourings they contain can easily overpower delicate dishes and they also tend to be very salty.

History

Soup was first made ten thousand years ago when the Egyptians prepared it by boiling ingredients in a large clay pot over an open fire and served it in shells or horns. Since then the popularity of soups has soared. Indeed, the Baulangers Inn in Paris, the forerunner of all restaurants, had nothing but soup on its menu. Today, the range of soups has widened vastly and cooking methods and recipes have completely changed. Soup, however, has continued to be an all-time favourite.

Most soups are very nutritious, especially those which have a high vegetable content, while being inexpensive and filling. In fact, these are the reasons why it has been served in soup kitchens for many years. Surprisingly perhaps, it was Al Capone who founded and funded the first soup kitchen as a charitable organisation in Chicago in the 1930s. He actually paid $350 per day from his own finances to feed as many as 3000 unemployed people. It has been suggested however, that his actions were motivated not by human kindness but rather by the fact that he wanted to prevent people revealing the secrets of his criminal activities.

International Specialities

Soup is generally extremely easy to make, as it is simply a process of boiling a combination of meats, fish or vegetables together to obtained the desired consistency. Certain soups, such as French Onion, have become renowned as national specialities.

Soup is very popular in Italy where key ingredients vary from region to region. In northern Italy soups are based on rice while in Tuscany thick bean or bread-based soups are popular. In southern Italy, tomato, garlic and pasta soups are favoured. Minestrone is perhaps the most well-known Italian soup and is now made world-wide with arguably the best version originating from Milan. As with elsewhere in the world, fish soups are often local specialities in Italy, the best ones being produced in coastal fishing villages.

Soup is an integral part of the Chinese meal but is more frequently served as a main course or to clear the palate between courses rather than as a starter.

Chinese soups are frequently clear but contain wontons, dumplings, noodles or rice to add texture and flavour.

Borscht originates from Eastern Europe and is particularly popular in Poland and Russia. Its popularity may be due in part to its vivid red colour caused by its main ingredient: beetroot. Borscht was introduced to France by Russian emigrants in the 1920s and has now become an established favourite. Various derivatives of the original Borscht have evolved to produce other quick, simple and healthy beetroot soups.

Perhaps the most famous of the French soups — aside from French Onion — is Vichyssoise. A popular favourite, it was originally a leek and potato soup created by a French chef working in America. It is usually served cold, thickened with fresh cream and garnished with chives. Today the term Vichyssoise is used to refer to any cold potato based soup made with another vegetable such as courgettes.

The Spanish also have a traditional soup called Gazpacho. Traditionally served ice-cold, it is made from cucumber, tomato, red pepper, bread crumbs, garlic and olive oil. Preparation varies between regions throughout Spain: in Jerez for example it served garnished with raw onions whereas in Cadiz it is served hot in winter.

The Naming of Soups

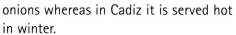

Although soup is great served hot to warm you up in the winter, some soups can be served cold (such as Vichyssoise or fruit soup) making them ideal for summer lunches or for light evening meals when served with a sandwich or salad. Garnishing with croutons, grated cheese or soured cream often enhances the flavour of the soup while also improving its presentation.

Bisque: made with puréed shellfish, fresh cream and Cognac. This dish evolved from a boiled game or meat soup to one made with pigeon or quail, until crayfish became established as the key ingredient in the seventeenth century.

Bouillabaisse: commonly associated with expensive restaurants, this dish was traditionally prepared on the beach by fisherman who boiled together scraps of unsaleable fish with herbs to form a hearty meal. The word *bouillabaisse* more correctly describes this form of cooking which means to boil rapidly and reduce. Almost any fish, including shellfish, can be used to make *bouillabaisse*, although oily fish such as sardines and mackerel should be avoided. Traditionally the soup and the fish are served separately with the soup poured over dried home-made bread. Today the bread is frequently replaced with garlic croutons.

Bouillon: now available as granules or ready made preparations, bouillon is the unclarified broth obtained by boiling meat or vegetables. It is used instead of water for preparing stocks and sauces.

Chowder: this is an American or Canadian name describing a clam or fish soup so thick it is almost a stew.

Consommé: formed from meat, fish or poultry stock, it can be served hot or cold. This clear soup can be garnished with thinly sliced meat, vermicelli, vegetables, bone marrow, poached eggs, cheese or croutons. Cold consommé may appear gelatinous, this is caused by the concentration of nutritive elements.

Gumbo: this soup originating from Louisiana is a particular favourite in North America and Canada. The okra pods traditionally used in its preparation serve to thicken the mixture so that the resultant dish is almost a stew.

Purée: this term is generally used to describe any thick soup where the ingredients have in part been blended or cooked until very soft. It is the starch from the puréed vegetables which thicken the soup.

Velouté: these are generally soups which have been thickened with egg yolks, butter and/or cream.

KEY

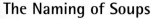 Simplicity level 1 – 3 (1 easiest, 3 slightly harder)

Preparation time

Cooking time

Thick Onion Soup

A delicious creamy soup with grated carrot and parsley for texture and colour. Serve with crusty cheese scones (biscuits) for a hearty lunch.

NUTRITIONAL INFORMATION

Calories 277   Sugars 12g
Protein . . . . .6g   Fat 20g
Carbohydrate . . .19g   Saturates 8g

 20 MINS   1HR 10 MINS

SERVES 6

I N G R E D I E N T S

75 g/2¾ oz/5 tbsp butter

500 g/1 lb 2 oz onions, finely chopped

1 garlic clove, crushed

40 g/1½ oz/6 tbsp plain (all-purpose) flour

600 ml/1 pint/2½ cups vegetable stock

600 ml/1 pint/2½ cups milk

2–3 tsp lemon or lime juice

good pinch of ground allspice

1 bay leaf

1 carrot, coarsely grated

4–6 tbsp double (heavy) cream

2 tbsp chopped parsley

salt and pepper

CHEESE SCONES (BISCUITS)

225 g/8 oz/2 cups malted wheat or
 wholemeal (whole wheat) flour

2 tsp baking powder

60 g/2 oz/¼ cup butter

4 tbsp grated Parmesan cheese

1 egg, beaten

about 75 ml/3 fl oz/⅓ cup milk

1 Melt the butter in a saucepan and fry the onions and garlic over a low heat, stirring frequently, for 10–15 minutes, until soft, but not coloured. Stir in the flour and cook, stirring, for 1 minute, then gradually stir in the stock and bring to the boil, stirring frequently. Add the milk, then bring back to the boil.

2 Season to taste with salt and pepper and add 2 teaspoons of the lemon or lime juice, the allspice and bay leaf. Cover and simmer for about 25 minutes until the vegetables are tender. Discard the bay leaf.

3 Meanwhile, make the scones (biscuits). Combine the flour, baking powder and seasoning and rub in the butter until the mixture resembles fine breadcrumbs. Stir in 3 tablespoons of the cheese, the egg and enough milk to mix to a soft dough.

4 Shape into a bar about 2 cm/¾ inch thick. Place on a floured baking tray (cookie sheet) and mark into slices. Sprinkle with the remaining cheese and bake in a preheated oven, 220°C/425°F/ Gas Mark 7, for about 20 minutes, until risen and golden brown.

5 Stir the carrot into the soup and simmer for 2–3 minutes. Add more lemon or lime juice, if necessary. Stir in the cream and reheat. Garnish and serve with the warm scones (biscuits).

Asparagus Soup

Fresh asparagus is now available for most of the year, so this soup can be made at any time. It can also be made using canned asparagus.

NUTRITIONAL INFORMATION

Calories	196	Sugars	.........7g
Protein	.........7g	Fat	..........12g
Carbohydrate	...15g	Saturates	.......4g

5–10 MINS   55 MINS

SERVES 6

I N G R E D I E N T S

1 bunch asparagus, about 350 g/12 oz,
  or 2 packs mini asparagus,
  about 150 g/5½ oz each

700 ml/1¼ pints/3 cups vegetable stock

60 g/2 oz/¼ cup butter or margarine

1 onion, chopped

3 tbsp plain (all-purpose) flour

¼ tsp ground coriander

1 tbsp lemon juice

450 ml/16 fl oz/2 cups milk

4–6 tbsp double (heavy) or single
  (light) cream

salt and pepper

1 Wash and trim the asparagus, discarding the woody part of the stem. Cut the remainder into short lengths, keeping a few tips for garnish. Mini asparagus does not need to be trimmed.

2 Cook the tips in the minimum of boiling salted water for 5–10 minutes. Drain and set aside.

3 Put the asparagus in a saucepan with the stock, bring to the boil, cover and simmer for about 20 minutes, until soft. Drain and reserve the stock.

4 Melt the butter or margarine in a saucepan. Add the onion and fry over a low heat until soft, but only barely coloured. Stir in the flour and cook for 1 minute, then gradually whisk in the reserved stock and bring to the boil.

5 Simmer for 2–3 minutes, until thickened, then stir in the cooked asparagus, seasoning, coriander and lemon juice. Simmer for 10 minutes, then cool a little and either press through a strainer or process in a blender or food processor until smooth.

6 Pour into a clean pan, add the milk and reserved asparagus tips and bring to the boil. Simmer for 2 minutes. Stir in the cream, reheat gently and serve.

COOK'S TIP

If using canned asparagus, drain off the liquid and use as part of the measured stock. Remove a few small asparagus tips for garnish and chop the remainder. Continue as above.

Beetroot (Beet) Soup

Here are two variations using the same vegetable: a creamy soup made with puréed cooked beetroot and a traditional clear soup, Bortscht.

NUTRITIONAL INFORMATION

Calories 106   Sugars 11g
Protein . . . . .3g   Fat 5g
Carbohydrate . . .13g   Saturates 3g

    25 MINS   35–55 MINS

SERVES 6

I N G R E D I E N T S

B O R T S C H

500 g/1 lb 2 oz raw beetroot (beets), peeled
  and grated

2 carrots, finely chopped

1 large onion, finely chopped

1 garlic clove, crushed

1 bouquet garni

1 litre/1¾ pints/5 cups vegetable stock

2–3 tsp lemon juice

salt and pepper

150 ml/¼ pint/⅔ cup soured cream, to serve

C R E A M E D   B E E T R O O T
(B E E T)   S O U P

60 g/2 oz/¼ cup butter or margarine

2 large onions, finely chopped

1–2 carrots, chopped

2 celery sticks, chopped

500 g/1 lb 2 oz cooked beetroot (beets), diced

1–2 tbsp lemon juice

900 ml/1½ pints/3½ cups vegetable stock

300 ml/½ pint/1¼ cups milk

salt and pepper

T O   S E R V E

grated cooked beetroot (beet) or 6 tbsp
  double (heavy) cream, lightly whipped

1 To make bortsch, place the beetroot (beets), carrots, onion, garlic, bouquet garni, stock and lemon juice in a saucepan and season to taste with salt and pepper. Bring to the boil, cover and simmer for 45 minutes.

2 Press the soup through a fine strainer or a strainer lined with muslin (cheesecloth), then pour into a clean pan. Taste and adjust the seasoning and add extra lemon juice, if necessary.

3 Bring to the boil and simmer for 1–2 minutes. Serve with a spoonful of soured cream swirled through.

4 To make creamed beetroot (beet) soup, melt the butter or margarine in a saucepan. Add the onions, carrots and celery and fry until just beginning to colour.

5 Add the beetroot (beet), 1 tablespoon of the lemon juice, the stock and seasoning and bring to the boil. Cover and simmer for 30 minutes, until tender.

6 Cool slightly, then press through a strainer or process in a food processor or blender. Pour into a clean pan. Add the milk and bring to the boil. Adjust the seasoning and add extra lemon juice, if necessary. Top with grated beetroot (beet) or double (heavy) cream.

Potato & Split Pea Soup

Split green peas are sweeter than other varieties of split pea and reduce down to a purée when cooked, which acts as a thickener in soups.

NUTRITIONAL INFORMATION

Calories 260   Sugars 5g
Protein ....11g   Fat 10g
Carbohydrate ...32g   Saturates 3g

 5–10 MINS   45 MINS

SERVES 4

I N G R E D I E N T S

2 tbsp vegetable oil

2 unpeeled floury (mealy) potatoes, diced

2 onions, diced

75 g/2¾ oz split green peas

1 litre/1¾ pints/4½ cups vegetable stock

5 tbsp grated Gruyère cheese

salt and pepper

C R O U T O N S

40 g/1½ oz/3 tbsp butter

1 garlic clove, crushed

1 tbsp chopped parsley

1 thick slice white bread, cubed

1 Heat the vegetable oil in a large saucepan. Add the potatoes and onions and sauté over a low heat, stirring constantly, for about 5 minutes.

VARIATION

For a richly coloured soup, red lentils could be used instead of split green peas. Add a large pinch of brown sugar to the recipe for extra sweetness if red lentils are used.

2 Add the split green peas to the pan and stir to mix together well.

3 Pour the vegetable stock into the pan and bring to the boil. Reduce the heat to low and simmer for 35 minutes, until the potatoes are tender and the split peas cooked.

4 Meanwhile, make the croûtons. Melt the butter in a frying pan (skillet). Add the garlic, parsley and bread cubes and cook, turning frequently, for about 2 minutes, until the bread cubes are golden brown on all sides.

5 Stir the grated cheese into the soup and season to taste with salt and pepper. Heat gently until the cheese is starting to melt.

6 Pour the soup into warmed individual bowls and sprinkle the croûtons on top. Serve at once.

Mushroom Noodle Soup

A light, refreshing clear soup of mushrooms, cucumber and small pieces of rice noodles, flavoured with soy sauce and a touch of garlic.

NUTRITIONAL INFORMATION

Calories 84   Sugars 1g
Protein . . . . .1g   Fat 8g
Carbohydrate . . . .3g   Saturates 1g

 5 MINS   10 MINS

SERVES 4

I N G R E D I E N T S

125 g/4½ oz flat or open-cup
  mushrooms

½ cucumber

2 spring onions (scallions)

1 garlic clove

2 tbsp vegetable oil

25 g/1 oz/¼ cup Chinese rice
  noodles

¾ tsp salt

1 tbsp soy sauce

1 Wash the mushrooms and pat dry on kitchen paper (paper towels). Slice thinly. Do not remove the peel as this adds more flavour.

2 Halve the cucumber lengthways. Scoop out the seeds, using a teaspoon, and slice the cucumber thinly.

3 Chop the spring onions (scallions) finely and cut the garlic clove into thin strips.

4 Heat the vegetable oil in a large saucepan or wok.

5 Add the spring onions (scallions) and garlic to the pan or wok and stir-fry for 30 seconds. Add the mushrooms and stir-fry for 2–3 minutes.

6 Stir in 600 ml/1 pint/2½ cups water. Break the noodles into short lengths and add to the soup. Bring to the boil, stirring occasionally.

7 Add the cucumber slices, salt and soy sauce, and simmer for 2–3 minutes.

8 Serve the mushroom noodle soup in warmed bowls, distributing the noodles and vegetables evenly.

COOK'S TIP

Scooping the seeds out from the cucumber gives it a prettier effect when sliced, and also helps to reduce any bitterness, but if you prefer, you can leave them in.

Avocado & Mint Soup

A rich and creamy pale green soup made with avocados and enhanced by a touch of chopped mint. Serve chilled in summer or hot in winter.

NUTRITIONAL INFORMATION

Calories 199	Sugars 3g	
Protein 3g	Fat 18g	
Carbohydrate 7g	Saturates 6g	

 15 MINS   35 MINS

SERVES 6

INGREDIENTS

40 g/1½ oz/3 tbsp butter or margarine

6 spring onions (scallions), sliced

1 garlic clove, crushed

25 g/1 oz/¼ cup plain (all-purpose) flour

600 ml/1 pint/2½ cups vegetable stock

2 ripe avocados

2–3 tsp lemon juice

pinch of grated lemon rind

150 ml/¼ pint/⅔ cup milk

150 ml/¼ pint/⅔ cup single (light) cream

1–1½ tbsp chopped mint

salt and pepper

mint sprigs, to garnish

MINTED GARLIC BREAD

125 g/4½ oz/½ cup butter

1–2 tbsp chopped mint

1–2 garlic cloves, crushed

1 wholemeal (whole wheat) or
    white French bread stick

1 Melt the butter or margarine in a large, heavy-based saucepan. Add the spring onions (scallions) and garlic clove and fry over a low heat, stirring occasionally, for about 3 minutes, until soft and translucent.

2 Stir in the flour and cook, stirring, for 1–2 minutes. Gradually stir in the stock, then bring to the boil. Simmer gently while preparing the avocados.

3 Peel the avocados, discard the stones (pits) and chop coarsely. Add to the soup with the lemon juice and rind and seasoning. Cover and simmer for about 10 minutes, until tender.

4 Cool the soup slightly, then press through a strainer with the back of a spoon or process in a food processor or blender until a smooth purée forms. Pour into a bowl.

5 Stir in the milk and cream, adjust the seasoning, then stir in the mint. Cover and chill thoroughly.

6 To make the minted garlic bread, soften the butter and beat in the mint and garlic. Cut the loaf into slanting slices but leave a hinge on the bottom crust. Spread each slice with the butter and reassemble the loaf. Wrap in foil and place in a preheated oven, 180°C/350°F/Gas Mark 4, for about 15 minutes.

7 Serve the soup garnished with a sprig of mint and accompanied by the minted garlic bread.

  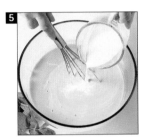

Stilton & Walnut Soup

Full of flavour, this rich and creamy soup is very simple to make and utterly delicious to eat.

NUTRITIONAL INFORMATION

Calories 392	Sugars 8g
Protein 15g	Fat 30g
Carbohydrate . . .15g	Saturates 16g

 10 MINS   30 MINS

SERVES 4

I N G R E D I E N T S

60 g/2 oz/4 tbsp butter

2 shallots, chopped

3 celery sticks, chopped

1 garlic clove, crushed

2 tbsp plain (all-purpose) flour

600 ml/1 pint/2½ cups vegetable stock

300 ml/½ pint/1¼ cups milk

150 g/5½ oz/1½ cups blue Stilton cheese, crumbled, plus extra to garnish

2 tbsp walnut halves, roughly chopped

150 ml/¼ pint/⅔ cup natural (unsweetened) yogurt

salt and pepper

chopped celery leaves, to garnish

1 Melt the butter in a large, heavy-based saucepan and sauté the shallots, celery and garlic, stirring occasionally, for 2–3 minutes, until softened.

2 Lower the heat, add the flour and cook, stirring constantly, for 30 seconds.

3 Gradually stir in the vegetable stock and milk and bring to the boil.

4 Reduce the heat to a gentle simmer and add the crumbled blue Stilton cheese and walnut halves. Cover and simmer for 20 minutes.

5 Stir in the yogurt and heat through for a further 2 minutes without boiling.

6 Season the soup to taste with salt and pepper, then transfer to a warm soup tureen or individual serving bowls, garnish with chopped celery leaves and extra crumbled blue Stilton cheese and serve at once.

COOK'S TIP

As well as adding protein, vitamins and useful fats to the diet, nuts add important flavour and texture to vegetarian meals.

Leek, Potato & Carrot Soup

A quick chunky soup, ideal for a snack or a quick lunch. The leftovers can be puréed to make one portion of creamed soup for the next day.

NUTRITIONAL INFORMATION

Calories 156	Sugars 7g
Protein 4g	Fat 6g
Carbohydrate ...22g	Saturates 0.7g

10 MINS   25 MINS

SERVES 2

INGREDIENTS

1 leek, about 175 g/6 oz

1 tbsp sunflower oil

1 garlic clove, crushed

700 ml/1¼ pints/3 cups vegetable stock

1 bay leaf

¼ tsp ground cumin

175 g/6 oz/1 cup potatoes, diced

125 g/4½ oz/1 cup coarsely grated carrot

salt and pepper

chopped parsley, to garnish

PUREED SOUP

5–6 tbsp milk

1–2 tbsp double (heavy) cream, crème fraîche or soured cream

 Trim off and discard some of the coarse green part of the leek, then slice thinly and rinse thoroughly in cold water. Drain well.

 Heat the sunflower oil in a heavy-based saucepan. Add the leek and garlic, and fry over a low heat for about 2–3 minutes, until soft, but barely coloured. Add the vegetable stock, bay leaf and cumin and season to taste with salt and pepper. Bring the mixture to the boil, stirring constantly.

3 Add the diced potato to the saucepan, cover and simmer over a low heat for 10–15 minutes until the potato is just tender, but not broken up.

4 Add the grated carrot and simmer for a further 2–3 minutes. Adjust the seasoning, discard the bay leaf and serve sprinkled liberally with chopped parsley.

5 To make a puréed soup, first process the leftovers (about half the original soup) in a blender or food processor or press through a strainer until smooth and then return to a clean saucepan with the milk. Bring to the boil and simmer for 2–3 minutes. Adjust the seasoning and stir in the cream or crème fraîche before serving sprinkled with chopped parsley.

Winter Soup

A thick vegetable soup which is a delicious meal in itself. Serve the soup with thin shavings of Parmesan and warm ciabatta bread.

NUTRITIONAL INFORMATION

Calories 285	Sugars 11g
Protein 16g	Fat 12g
Carbohydrate . . .29g	Saturates 3g

 10 MINS   20 MINS

SERVES 4

INGREDIENTS

2 tbsp olive oil

2 leeks, thinly sliced

2 courgettes (zucchini), chopped

2 garlic cloves, crushed

2 x 400 g/14 oz cans chopped tomatoes

1 tbsp tomato purée (paste)

1 bay leaf

900 ml/1½ pints/3¾ cups vegetable stock

400 g/14 oz can chickpeas (garbanzo
    beans), drained

225 g/8 oz spinach

25 g/1 oz Parmesan cheese,
    thinly shaved

salt and pepper

crusty bread, to serve

1 Heat the oil in a heavy-based saucepan. Add the sliced leeks and courgettes (zucchini) and cook over a medium heat, stirring constantly, for 5 minutes.

2 Add the garlic, chopped tomatoes, tomato purée (paste), bay leaf, vegetable stock and chickpeas (garbanzo beans). Bring to the boil, lower the heat and simmer, stirring occasionally, for 5 minutes.

3 Shred the spinach finely, add to the soup and boil for 2 minutes. Season to taste with salt and pepper.

4 Remove the bay leaf. Pour into a soup tureen and sprinkle over the Parmesan. Serve with crusty bread.

Plum Tomato Soup

Homemade tomato soup is easy to make and always tastes better than bought varieties. Try this version with its Mediterranean influences.

NUTRITIONAL INFORMATION

Calories 402	Sugars 14g
Protein 7g	Fat 32g
Carbohydrate ...16g	Saturates 3g

 20 MINS   30–35 MINS

SERVES 4

I N G R E D I E N T S

2 tbsp olive oil

2 red onions, chopped

2 celery sticks, chopped

1 carrot, chopped

500 g/1 lb 2 oz plum tomatoes, halved

750 ml/1¼ pints/3 cups vegetable stock

1 tbsp chopped oregano

1 tbsp chopped basil

150 ml/¼ pint/⅔ cup dry white wine

2 tsp caster (superfine) sugar

125 g/4½ oz/1 cup hazelnuts, toasted

125 g/4½ oz/1 cup black or green olives

handful of basil leaves

1 tbsp olive oil

1 loaf ciabatta bread (Italian-style loaf)

salt and pepper

basil sprigs to garnish

1 Heat the oil in a large saucepan. Add the onions, celery and carrot and fry over a low heat, stirring frequently, until softened, but not coloured.

2 Add the tomatoes, stock, chopped herbs, wine and sugar. Bring to the boil, cover and simmer for 20 minutes.

3 Place the toasted hazelnuts in a blender or food processor, together with the olives and basil leaves and process until thoroughly combined, but not too smooth. Alternatively, finely chop the nuts, olives and basil leaves and pound them together in a mortar with a pestle, then turn into a small bowl. Add the olive oil and process or beat thoroughly for a few seconds. Turn the mixture into a serving bowl.

4 Warm the ciabatta bread in a preheated oven, 190°C/375°F/ Gas Mark 5, for 3–4 minutes.

5 Process the soup in a blender or a food processor, or press through a strainer, until smooth, Check the seasoning. Ladle into warmed soup bowls and garnish with sprigs of basil. Slice the warm bread and spread with the olive and hazelnut paste. Serve with the soup.

Spinach & Mascarpone Soup

Spinach is the basis for this delicious soup, which has creamy mascarpone cheese stirred through it to give it a wonderful texture.

NUTRITIONAL INFORMATION

Calories 402	Sugars 2g
Protein 11g	Fat 36g
Carbohydrate . . .10g	Saturates 21g

 15 MINS   30 MINS

SERVES 4

INGREDIENTS

60 g/2 oz/¼ cup butter

1 bunch spring onions (scallions),
   trimmed and chopped

2 celery sticks, chopped

350 g/12 oz/3 cups spinach or sorrel, or
   3 bunches watercress

850 ml /1½ pints/3½ cups vegetable stock

225 g/8 oz/1 cup mascarpone cheese

1 tbsp olive oil

2 slices thick-cut bread, cut into cubes

½ tsp caraway seeds

salt and pepper

sesame bread sticks, to serve

1 Melt half the butter in a very large saucepan. Add the spring onions (scallions) and celery, and cook over a medium heat, stirring frequently, for about 5 minutes, until softened.

2 Pack the spinach, sorrel or watercress into the saucepan. Add the stock and bring to the boil, then reduce the heat, cover and simmer for 15–20 minutes.

3 Transfer the soup to a blender or food processor and process until smooth. Alternatively, rub it through a strainer. Return to the saucepan.

4 Add the mascarpone to the soup and heat gently, stirring constantly, until smooth and blended. Season to taste with salt and pepper.

5 Heat the remaining butter with the oil in a frying pan (skillet). Add the bread cubes and fry, turning frequently, until golden brown, adding the caraway seeds towards the end of cooking, so that they do not burn.

6 Ladle the soup into warmed bowls. Sprinkle with the croûtons and serve with the sesame bread sticks.

VARIATION

Any leafy vegetable can be used to make this soup to give variations to the flavour. For anyone who grows their own vegetables, it is the perfect recipe for experimenting with a glut of produce. Try young beetroot (beet) leaves or surplus lettuces for a change.

Broad (Fava) Bean Soup

Fresh broad (fava) beans are best for this scrumptious soup, but if they are unavailable, use frozen beans instead.

NUTRITIONAL INFORMATION

Calories 224	Sugars 4g
Protein 12g	Fat 6g
Carbohydrate . . .31g	Saturates 1g

 15 MINS   40 MINS

SERVES 4

INGREDIENTS

2 tbsp olive oil

1 red onion, chopped

2 garlic cloves, crushed

2 potatoes, diced

500 g/1 lb 2 oz/3 cups broad (fava) beans,
   thawed if frozen

850 ml/1½ pints/3¾ cups vegetable stock

2 tbsp freshly chopped mint

mint sprigs and natural
   (unsweetened) yogurt, to garnish

1 Heat the olive oil in a large saucepan. Add the onion and garlic and sauté for 2–3 minutes, until softened.

2 Add the potatoes and cook, stirring constantly, for 5 minutes.

3 Stir in the beans and the stock, cover and simmer for 30 minutes, or until the beans and potatoes are tender.

4 Remove a few vegetables with a slotted spoon and set aside until required. Place the remainder of the soup in a food processor or blender and process until smooth.

5 Return the soup to a clean saucepan and add the reserved vegetables and chopped mint. Stir thoroughly and heat through gently.

6 Transfer the soup to a warm tureen or individual serving bowls. Garnish with swirls of yogurt and sprigs of fresh mint and serve immediately.

 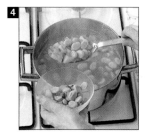 

VARIATION

Use fresh coriander (cilantro) and ½ tsp ground cumin as flavourings in the soup, if you prefer.

Cream Cheese & Herb Soup

Make the most of home-grown herbs to create this wonderfully creamy soup with its marvellous garden-fresh fragrance.

NUTRITIONAL INFORMATION

Calories 275	Sugars 5g	
Protein 7g	Fat 22g	
Carbohydrate . . .14g	Saturates 11g	

   15 MINS   35 MINS

SERVES 4

INGREDIENTS

25 g/1 oz/2 tbsp butter or margarine

2 onions, chopped

850 ml/1½ pints/3½ cups vegetable stock

25 g/1 oz coarsely chopped mixed
    herbs, such as parsley, chives, thyme,
    basil and oregano

200 g/7 oz/1 cup full-fat soft cheese

1 tbsp cornflour (cornstarch)

1 tbsp milk

chopped chives, to garnish

1 Melt the butter or margarine in a large, heavy-based saucepan. Add the onions and fry over a medium heat for 2 minutes, then cover and turn the heat to low. Continue to cook the onions for 5 minutes, then remove the lid.

2 Add the vegetable stock and herbs to the saucepan. Bring to the boil over a moderate heat. Lower the heat, cover and simmer gently for 20 minutes.

3 Remove the saucepan from the heat. Transfer the soup to a food processor or blender and process for about 15 seconds, until smooth. Alternatively, press it through a strainer with the back of a wooden spoon. Return the soup to the saucepan.

4 Reserve a little of the cheese for garnish. Spoon the remaining cheese into the soup and whisk until it has melted and is incorporated.

5 Mix the cornflour (cornstarch) with the milk to a paste, then stir the mixture into the soup. Heat, stirring constantly, until thickened and smooth.

6 Pour the soup into warmed individual bowls. Spoon some of the reserved cheese into each bowl and garnish with chives. Serve at once.

Avocado & Vegetable Soup

Avocado has a rich flavour and colour which makes a creamy flavoured soup. It is best served chilled, but may be eaten warm as well.

NUTRITIONAL INFORMATION

Calories	167	Sugars	.........5g
Protein	.........4g	Fat	..........13g
Carbohydrate	....8g	Saturates	.......3g

 15 MINS   10 MINS

SERVES 4

I N G R E D I E N T S

1 large, ripe avocado

2 tbsp lemon juice

1 tbsp vegetable oil

50 g/1¾ oz/½ cup canned
  sweetcorn (corn), drained

2 tomatoes, peeled and seeded

1 garlic clove, crushed

1 leek, chopped

1 red chilli, chopped

425 ml/¾ pint/2 cups vegetable stock

150 ml/¼ pint/⅔ cup milk

shredded leek, to garnish

1 Peel the avocado and mash the flesh with a fork, stir in the lemon juice and reserve until required.

2 Heat the oil in a large saucepan. Add the sweetcorn (corn), tomatoes, garlic, leek and chilli and sauté over a low heat for 2–3 minutes, or until the vegetables have softened.

3 Put half the vegetable mixture in a food processor or blender, together with the mashed avocado and process until smooth. Transfer the mixture to a clean saucepan.

4 Add the vegetable stock, milk and reserved vegetables and cook over a low heat for 3–4 minutes, until hot. Transfer to warmed individual serving bowls, garnish with shredded leek and serve immediately.

COOK'S TIP

If serving chilled, transfer from the food processor to a bowl, stir in the vegetable stock and milk, cover and chill in the refrigerator for at least 4 hours.

Broccoli & Potato Soup

This creamy soup has a delightful pale green colouring and rich flavour from the blend of tender broccoli and blue cheese.

NUTRITIONAL INFORMATION

Calories	452	Sugars	.........4g
Protein	........14g	Fat	..........35g
Carbohydrate	...20g	Saturates	......19g

 5–10 MINS   40 MINS

SERVES 4

INGREDIENTS

2 tbsp olive oil

2 potatoes, diced

1 onion, diced

225 g/8 oz broccoli florets

125 g/4½ oz blue cheese, crumbled

1 litre/1¾ pints/4½ cups vegetable stock

150 ml/¼ pint/⅔ cup double (heavy) cream

pinch of paprika

salt and pepper

1 Heat the oil in a large saucepan. Add the potatoes and onion. Sauté, stirring constantly, for 5 minutes.

2 Reserve a few broccoli florets for the garnish and add the remaining broccoli to the pan. Add the cheese and vegetable stock.

COOK'S TIP

This soup freezes very successfully. Follow the method described here up to step 4, and freeze the soup after it has been puréed. Add the cream and paprika just before serving. Garnish and serve.

3 Bring to the boil, then reduce the heat, cover the pan and simmer for 25 minutes, until the potatoes are tender.

4 Transfer the soup to a food processor or blender in batches and process until the mixture is smooth. Alternatively, press the vegetables through a strainer with the back of a wooden spoon.

5 Return the purée to a clean saucepan and stir in the double (heavy) cream and a pinch of paprika. Season to taste with salt and pepper.

6 Blanch the reserved broccoli florets in a little boiling water for about 2 minutes, then lift them out of the pan with a slotted spoon.

7 Pour the soup into warmed individual bowls and garnish with the broccoli florets and a sprinkling of paprika. Serve immediately.

Spanish Tomato Soup

This Mediterranean tomato soup is thickened with bread, as is traditional in some parts of Spain, and served with garlic bread.

NUTRITIONAL INFORMATION

Calories 297	Sugars 7g
Protein 8g	Fat 13g
Carbohydrate ...39g	Saturates 2g

 10 MINS 20 MINS

SERVES 4

I N G R E D I E N T S

4 tbsp olive oil

1 onion, chopped

3 garlic cloves, crushed

1 green (bell) pepper, seeded and chopped

½ tsp chilli powder

500 g/1 lb 2 oz tomatoes, chopped

225 g/8 oz French or Italian bread, cubed

1 litre/1¾ pints/4 cups vegetable stock

GARLIC BREAD

4 slices ciabatta or French bread

4 tbsp olive oil

2 garlic cloves, crushed

25 g/1 oz/¼ cup grated Cheddar cheese

chilli powder, to garnish

1 Heat the olive oil in a large frying pan (skillet). Add the onion, garlic and (bell) pepper and sauté over a low heat, stirring frequently, for 2–3 minutes, or until the onion has softened.

2 Add the chilli powder and tomatoes and cook over a medium heat until the mixture has thickened.

3 Stir in the bread cubes and stock and cook for 10–15 minutes, until the soup is thick and fairly smooth.

4 Meanwhile, make the garlic bread. Toast the bread slices under a medium grill (broiler). Drizzle the oil over the top of the bread, rub with the garlic, sprinkle with the cheese and return to the grill (broiler) for 2–3 minutes, until the cheese has melted. Sprinkle with chilli powder and serve with the soup.

VARIATION

Replace the green (bell) pepper with red or orange (bell) pepper, if you prefer.

Cauliflower & Broccoli Soup

Full of flavour, this creamy cauliflower and broccoli soup is simple to make and absolutely delicious to eat.

NUTRITIONAL INFORMATION

Calories 378   Sugars 14g
Protein . . . . .18g   Fat 26g
Carbohydrate . . .20g   Saturates 7g

  10 MINS   35 MINS

SERVES 4

I N G R E D I E N T S

3 tbsp vegetable oil

1 red onion, chopped

2 garlic cloves, crushed

300 g/10½ oz cauliflower florets

300 g/10½ oz broccoli florets

1 tbsp plain (all-purpose) flour

600 ml/1 pint/2½ cups milk

300 ml/½ pint/1¼ cups vegetable stock

75 g/2¾ oz/¾ cup Gruyère cheese, grated

pinch of paprika

150 ml/¼ pint/⅔ cup single (light) cream

paprika and Gruyère cheese shavings,
   to garnish

1 Heat the oil in a large, heavy-based saucepan. Add the onion, garlic, cauliflower florets and broccoli florets and sauté over a low heat, stirring constantly, for 3–4 minutes. Add the flour and cook, stirring constantly for a further 1 minute.

2 Gradually stir in the milk and stock and bring to the boil, stirring constantly. Reduce the heat and simmer for 20 minutes.

3 Remove about a quarter of the vegetables with a slotted spoon and set aside. Put the remaining soup in a food processor or blender and process for about 30 seconds, until smooth. Alternatively, press the vegetables through a strainer with the back of a wooden spoon. Transfer the soup to a clean saucepan.

4 Return the reserved vegetable pieces to the soup. Stir in the grated cheese, paprika and single (light) cream and heat through over a low heat, without boiling, for 2–3 minutes, or until the cheese starts to melt.

5 Transfer to warmed individual serving bowls, garnish with shavings of Gruyère and dust with paprika and serve immediately.

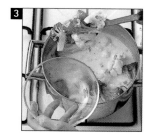

COOK'S TIP

The soup must not start to boil after the cream has been added, otherwise it will curdle. Use natural (unsweetened) yogurt instead of the cream if preferred, but again do not allow it to boil.

Curried Parsnip Soup

Parsnips make a delicious soup as they have a slightly sweet flavour. In this recipe, spices are added to complement this sweetness.

NUTRITIONAL INFORMATION

Calories 152   Sugars 7g
Protein ....3g   Fat 8g
Carbohydrate ...18g   Saturates 3g

 10 MINS   35 MINS

SERVES 4

I N G R E D I E N T S

1 tbsp vegetable oil

15 g/½ oz/1 tbsp butter

1 red onion, chopped

3 parsnips, chopped

2 garlic cloves, crushed

2 tsp garam masala

½ tsp chilli powder

1 tbsp plain (all-purpose) flour

850 ml/1½ pints/3¾ cups vegetable stock

grated rind and juice of 1 lemon

salt and pepper

lemon rind, to garnish

1 Heat the oil and butter in a large saucepan until the butter has melted. Add the onion, parsnips and garlic and sauté, stirring frequently, for about 5–7 minutes, until the vegetables have softened, but not coloured.

2 Add the garam masala and chilli powder and cook, stirring constantly, for 30 seconds. Sprinkle in the flour, mixing well and cook, stirring constantly, for a further 30 seconds.

3 Stir in the stock, lemon rind and juice and bring to the boil. Reduce the heat and simmer for 20 minutes.

4 Remove some of the vegetable pieces with a slotted spoon and reserve until required. Process the remaining soup and vegetables in a food processor or blender for about 1 minute, or until a smooth purée. Alternatively, press the vegetables through a strainer with the back of a wooden spoon.

5 Return the soup to a clean saucepan and stir in the reserved vegetables. Heat the soup through for 2 minutes until piping hot.

6 Season to taste with salt and pepper, then transfer to soup bowls, garnish with grated lemon rind and serve.

Vichyssoise

This is a classic creamy soup made from potatoes and leeks. To achieve the delicate pale colour, be sure to use only the white parts of the leeks.

NUTRITIONAL INFORMATION

Calories 208   Sugars 5g
Protein . . . . .5g   Fat 12g
Carbohydrate . . .20g   Saturates 6g

10 MINS   40 MINS

SERVES 6

INGREDIENTS

3 large leeks

40 g/1½ oz/3 tbsp butter or margarine

1 onion, thinly sliced

500 g/1 lb 2 oz potatoes, chopped

850 ml/1½ pints/3½ cups vegetable stock

2 tsp lemon juice

pinch of ground nutmeg

¼ tsp ground coriander

1 bay leaf

1 egg yolk

150 ml/¼ pint/⅔ cup single (light) cream

salt and white pepper

TO GARNISH

freshly snipped chives

1 Trim the leeks and remove most of the green part. Slice the white part of the leeks very finely.

2 Melt the butter or margarine in a saucepan. Add the leeks and onion and fry, stirring occasionally, for about 5 minutes without browning.

3 Add the potatoes, vegetable stock, lemon juice, nutmeg, coriander and bay leaf to the pan, season to taste with salt and pepper and bring to the boil. Cover and simmer for about 30 minutes, until all the vegetables are very soft.

4 Cool the soup a little, remove and discard the bay leaf and then press through a strainer or process in a food processor or blender until smooth. Pour into a clean pan.

5 Blend the egg yolk into the cream, add a little of the soup to the mixture and then whisk it all back into the soup and reheat gently, without boiling. Adjust the seasoning to taste. Cool and then chill thoroughly in the refrigerator.

6 Serve the soup sprinkled with freshly snipped chives.

Speedy Beetroot (Beet) Soup

Quick and easy to prepare in a microwave oven, this deep red soup of puréed beetroot (beets) and potatoes makes a stunning first course.

NUTRITIONAL INFORMATION

Calories 120	Sugars 11g
Protein 4g	Fat 2g
Carbohydrate ...22g	Saturates 1g

 20 MINS   30 MINS

SERVES 6

INGREDIENTS

1 onion, chopped

350 g/12 oz potatoes, diced

1 small cooking apple, peeled,
    cored and grated

3 tbsp water

1 tsp cumin seeds

500 g/1 lb 2 oz cooked beetroot (beets),
    peeled and diced

1 bay leaf

pinch of dried thyme

1 tsp lemon juice

600 ml/1 pint/2½ cups hot vegetable stock

4 tbsp soured cream

salt and pepper

few dill sprigs, to garnish

1 Place the onion, potatoes, apple and water in a large bowl. Cover and cook in the microwave on HIGH power for 10 minutes.

2 Stir in the cumin seeds and cook on HIGH power for 1 minute.

3 Stir in the beetroot (beets), bay leaf, thyme, lemon juice and hot vegetable stock. Cover and microwave on HIGH power for 12 minutes, stirring halfway through the cooking time.

4 Leave to stand, uncovered, for 5 minutes. Remove and discard the bay leaf. Strain the vegetables and reserve the liquid. Process the vegetables with a little of the reserved liquid in a food processor or blender until they are smooth and creamy. Alternatively, either mash the vegetables with a potato masher or press them through a strainer with the back of a wooden spoon.

5 Pour the vegetable purée into a clean bowl with the reserved liquid and mix well. Season to taste. Cover and microwave on HIGH power for 4–5 minutes, until the soup is piping hot.

6 Serve the soup in warmed bowls. Swirl 1 tablespoon of soured cream into each serving and garnish with a few sprigs of fresh dill.

Gardener's Broth

This hearty soup uses a variety of green vegetables with a flavouring of ground coriander. A finishing touch of thinly sliced leeks adds texture.

NUTRITIONAL INFORMATION

Calories	 169	Sugars	.... 5g
Protein	.... 4g	Fat	.... 13g
Carbohydrate	.... 8g	Saturates	.... 5g

 10 MINS   45 MINS

SERVES 6

INGREDIENTS

40 g/1½ oz/3 tbsp butter

1 onion, chopped

1–2 garlic cloves, crushed

1 large leek

225 g/8 oz Brussels sprouts

125 g/4½ oz French (green) or runner (string) beans

1.2 litres/2 pints/5 cups vegetable stock

125 g/4½ oz/1 cup frozen peas

1 tbsp lemon juice

½ tsp ground coriander

4 tbsp double (heavy) cream

salt and pepper

MELBA TOAST

4–6 slices white bread

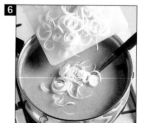

1 Melt the butter in a saucepan. Add the onion and garlic and fry over a low heat, stirring occasionally, until they begin to soften, but not colour.

2 Slice the white part of the leek very thinly and reserve; slice the remaining leek. Slice the Brussels sprouts and thinly slice the beans.

3 Add the green part of the leeks, the Brussels sprouts and beans to the saucepan. Add the stock and bring to the boil. Simmer for 10 minutes.

4 Add the frozen peas, seasoning, lemon juice and coriander and continue to simmer for 10–15 minutes, until the vegetables are tender.

5 Cool the soup a little, then press through a strainer or process in a food processor or blender until smooth. Pour into a clean pan.

6 Add the reserved slices of leek to the soup, bring back to the boil and simmer for about 5 minutes, until the leek is tender. Adjust the seasoning, stir in the cream and reheat gently.

7 To make the melba toast, toast the bread on both sides under a preheated grill (broiler). Cut horizontally through the slices, then toast the uncooked sides until they curl up. Serve immediately with the soup.

Vegetable & Corn Chowder

This is a really filling soup, which should be served before a light main course. It is easy to prepare and filled with flavour.

NUTRITIONAL INFORMATION

Calories	378	Sugars	........20g
Protein	........16g	Fat	..........13g
Carbohydrate	...52g	Saturates	.......6g

  15 MINS   30 MINS

SERVES 4

I N G R E D I E N T S

1 tbsp vegetable oil

1 red onion, diced

1 red (bell) pepper, seeded and diced

3 garlic cloves, crushed

1 large potato, diced

2 tbsp plain (all-purpose) flour

600 ml/1 pint/2½ cups milk

300 ml/½ pint/1¼ cups vegetable stock

50 g/1¾ oz broccoli florets

300 g/10½ oz/3 cups canned
    sweetcorn (corn), drained

75 g/2¾ oz/¾ cup Cheddar cheese, grated

salt and pepper

1 tbsp chopped coriander (cilantro),
    to garnish

COOK'S TIP

Vegetarian cheeses are made with rennets of non-animal origin, using microbial or fungal enzymes.

1 Heat the oil in a large saucepan. Add the onion, (bell) pepper, garlic and potato and sauté over a low heat, stirring frequently, for 2–3 minutes.

2 Stir in the flour and cook, stirring for 30 seconds. Gradually stir in the milk and stock.

3 Add the broccoli and sweetcorn (corn). Bring the mixture to the boil, stirring constantly, then reduce the heat and simmer for about 20 minutes, or until all the vegetables are tender.

4 Stir in 50 g/1¾ oz/½ cup of the cheese until it melts.

5 Season and spoon the chowder into a warm soup tureen. Garnish with the remaining cheese and the coriander (cilantro) and serve.

Minted Pea & Yogurt Soup

A deliciously refreshing, summery soup that is full of goodness. It is also extremely tasty served chilled.

NUTRITIONAL INFORMATION

Calories	208	Sugars	.........9g
Protein	........10g	Fat	..........7g
Carbohydrate	...26g	Saturates	.......2g

 15 MINS 25 MINS

SERVES 6

I N G R E D I E N T S

2 tbsp vegetable ghee or sunflower oil

2 onions, coarsely chopped

225 g/8 oz potato, coarsely chopped

2 garlic cloves, crushed

2.5 cm/1 inch root ginger, chopped

1 tsp ground coriander

1 tsp ground cumin

1 tbsp plain (all-purpose) flour

850 ml/1½ pints/3½ cups vegetable stock

500 g/1 lb 2 oz frozen peas

2-3 tbsp chopped mint

salt and pepper

150 ml/¼ pint/⅔ cup strained
    Greek yogurt, plus extra to serve

½ tsp cornflour (cornstarch)

300 ml/½ pint/1¼ cups milk

mint sprigs, to garnish

1 Heat the vegetable ghee or sunflower oil in a saucepan, add the onions and potato and cook over a low heat, stirring occasionally, for about 3 minutes, until the onion is soft and translucent.

2 Stir in the garlic, ginger, coriander, cumin and flour and cook, stirring constantly, for 1 minute.

3 Add the vegetable stock, peas and the chopped mint and bring to the boil, stirring. Reduce the heat, cover and simmer gently for 15 minutes, or until the vegetables are tender.

4 Process the soup, in batches, in a blender or food processor. Return the mixture to the pan and season with salt and pepper to taste. Blend the yogurt with the cornflour (cornstarch) to a smooth paste and stir into the soup.

5 Add the milk and bring almost to the boil, stirring constantly. Cook very gently for 2 minutes. Serve the soup hot, garnished with the mint sprigs and a swirl of extra yogurt.

Potato & Pesto Soup

Fresh pesto is a treat to the taste buds and very different in flavour from that available from supermarkets. Store fresh pesto in the refrigerator.

NUTRITIONAL INFORMATION

Calories 548	Sugars 0g	
Protein 11g	Fat 52g	
Carbohydrate ...10g	Saturates 18g	

5–10 MINS   50 MINS

SERVES 4

I N G R E D I E N T S

3 slices rindless, smoked, fatty bacon

450 g/1 lb floury potatoes

450 g/ 1 lb onions

2 tbsp olive oil

25 g/1 oz/2 tbsp butter

600 ml/1 pint/2 ½ cups chicken stock

600 ml/1 pint/2 ½ cups milk

100 g/3 ½ oz/ ¾ cup dried conchigliette

150 ml/ ¼ pint/ ⅝ cup double (heavy) cream

chopped fresh parsley

salt and pepper

freshly grated Parmesan cheese and garlic

　bread, to serve

P E S T O   S A U C E

60 g/2 oz/1 cup finely chopped fresh

　parsley

2 garlic cloves, crushed

60 g/2 oz/ ⅔ cup pine nuts (kernels),

　crushed

2 tbsp chopped fresh basil leaves

60 g/2 oz/ ⅔ cup freshly grated Parmesan

　cheese

white pepper

150 ml/ ¼ pint/ ⅝ cup olive oil

1 To make the pesto sauce, put all of the ingredients in a blender or food processor and process for 2 minutes, or blend by hand using a pestle and mortar.

2 Finely chop the bacon, potatoes and onions. Fry the bacon in a large pan over a medium heat for 4 minutes. Add the butter, potatoes and onions and cook for 12 minutes, stirring constantly.

3 Add the stock and milk to the pan, bring to the boil and simmer for 10 minutes. Add the conchigliette and simmer for a further 10-12 minutes.

4 Blend in the cream and simmer for 5 minutes. Add the parsley, salt and pepper and 2 tbsp pesto sauce. Transfer the soup to serving bowls and serve with Parmesan cheese and fresh garlic bread.

Hot & Sour Mushroom Soup

Hot and sour soups are found across South East Asia in different forms. Reduce the number of chillies added if you prefer a milder dish.

NUTRITIONAL INFORMATION

Calories 87	Sugars 7g	
Protein 4g	Fat 5g	
Carbohydrate 8g	Saturates 1g	

 10 MINS   20 MINS

SERVES 4

I N G R E D I E N T S

2 tbsp tamarind paste

4 red chilies, very finely chopped

2 cloves garlic, crushed

2.5 cm/1 inch piece of Thai ginger, peeled and very finely chopped

4 tbsp fish sauce

2 tbsp palm sugar or caster (superfine) sugar

8 lime leaves, roughly torn

1.2 litres/2 pints/5 cups vegetable stock

100 g/3½ oz carrots, very thinly sliced

225 g/8 oz button mushrooms, halved

350 g/12 oz shredded white cabbage

100 g/3½ oz fine green beans, halved

3 tbsp fresh coriander (cilantro), roughly chopped

100 g/3½ oz cherry tomatoes, halved

COOK'S TIP

Tamarind is the dried fruit of the tamarind tree. Sold as a pulp or paste, it is used to give a special sweet and sour flavour to Oriental dishes.

1 Place the tamarind paste, red chillies, garlic, Thai ginger, fish sauce, palm or caster (superfine) sugar, lime leaves and vegetable stock in a large preheated wok or heavy-based frying pan (skillet). Bring the mixture to the boil, stirring occasionally.

2 Reduce the heat and add the carrots, mushrooms, white cabbage and green beans. Leave the soup to simmer, uncovered, for about 10 minutes, or until the vegetables are just tender.

3 Stir the fresh coriander (cilantro) and cherry tomatoes into the mixture in the wok and heat through for another 5 minutes.

4 Transfer the soup to a warm tureen or individual serving bowls and serve immediately.

Tuscan Onion Soup

This soup is best made with white onions, which have a mild flavour. If you cannot get hold of them, try using large Spanish onions instead.

NUTRITIONAL INFORMATION

Calories .... .390   Sugars 0g
Protein .... .9g   Fat 33g
Carbohydrate ...15g   Saturates ..... .14g

 5–10 MINS   40–45 MINS

SERVES 4

I N G R E D I E N T S

50 g/1¾ oz pancetta ham, diced

1 tbsp olive oil

4 large white onions, sliced thinly into rings

3 garlic cloves, chopped

850 ml/1½ pints/3½ cups hot chicken or
  ham stock

4 slices ciabatta or other Italian bread

50 g/1¾ oz/3 tbsp butter

75 g/2¾ oz Gruyère or Cheddar

salt and pepper

1 Dry fry the pancetta in a large saucepan for 3–4 minutes until it begins to brown. Remove the pancetta from the pan and set aside until required.

2 Add the oil to the pan and cook the onions and garlic over a high heat for 4 minutes. Reduce the heat, cover and cook for 15 minutes or until the onions are lightly caramelized.

3 Add the stock to the saucepan and bring to the boil. Reduce the heat and leave the mixture to simmer, covered, for about 10 minutes.

4 Toast the slices of ciabatta on both sides, under a preheated grill (broiler), for 2–3 minutes or until golden. Spread the ciabatta with butter and top with the Gruyère or Cheddar cheese. Cut the bread into bite-size pieces.

5 Add the reserved pancetta to the soup and season with salt and pepper to taste.

6 Pour into 4 soup bowls and top with the toasted bread.

COOK'S TIP

Pancetta is similar to bacon, but it is air- and salt-cured for about 6 months. Pancetta is available from most delicatessens and some large supermarkets. If you cannot obtain pancetta use unsmoked bacon instead.

Cream of Artichoke Soup

A creamy soup with the unique, subtle flavouring of Jerusalem artichokes and a garnish of grated carrots for extra crunch.

NUTRITIONAL INFORMATION

Calories	19	Sugars	.........0g
Protein	........0.4g	Fat	...........2g
Carbohydrate	...0.7g	Saturates	.....0.7g

 10–15 MINS 55–60 MINS

SERVES 6

I N G R E D I E N T S

750 g/1 lb 10 oz Jerusalem artichokes

1 lemon, sliced thickly

60 g/2 oz/¼ cup butter or margarine

2 onions, chopped

1 garlic clove, crushed

1.25 litres/2¼ pints/5½ cups chicken or
   vegetable stock

2 bay leaves

¼ tsp ground mace or ground nutmeg

1 tbsp lemon juice

150 ml/¼ pint/⅔ cup single (light) cream or
   natural fromage frais

salt and pepper

TO GARNISH

coarsely grated carrot

chopped fresh parsley or coriander
   (cilantro)

1 Peel and slice the artichokes. Put into a bowl of water with the lemon slices.

2 Melt the butter or margarine in a large saucepan. Add the onions and garlic and fry gently for 3–4 minutes until soft but not coloured.

3 Drain the artichokes (discarding the lemon) and add to the pan. Mix well and cook gently for 2–3 minutes without allowing to colour.

4 Add the stock, seasoning, bay leaves, mace or nutmeg and lemon juice. Bring slowly to the boil, then cover and simmer gently for about 30 minutes until the vegetables are very tender.

5 Discard the bay leaves. Cool the soup slightly then press through a sieve (strainer) or blend in a food processor until smooth. If liked, a little of the soup may be only partially puréed and added to the rest of the puréed soup, to give extra texture.

6 Pour into a clean pan and bring to the boil. Adjust the seasoning and stir in the cream or fromage frais. Reheat gently without boiling. Garnish with grated carrot and chopped parsley or coriander (cilantro).

Vegetable & Bean Soup

This wonderful combination of cannellini beans, vegetables and vermicelli is made even richer by the addition of pesto and dried mushrooms.

NUTRITIONAL INFORMATION

Calories	294	Sugars	.........2g
Protein	........11g	Fat	..........16g
Carbohydrate	...30g	Saturates	.......2g

 30 MINS   30 MINS

SERVES 4

I N G R E D I E N T S

1 small aubergine (eggplant)

2 large tomatoes

1 potato, peeled

1 carrot, peeled

1 leek

425 g/15 oz can cannellini beans

850 ml/1½ pints/3¾ cups hot vegetable or
   chicken stock

2 tsp dried basil

15 g/½ oz dried porcini mushrooms,
   soaked for 10 minutes in enough warm
   water to cover

50 g/1¾ oz/¼ cup vermicelli

3 tbsp pesto

freshly grated Parmesan cheese, to serve
   (optional)

1 Slice the aubergine (eggplant) into rings about 1 cm/½ inch thick, then cut each ring into 4.

2 Cut the tomatoes and potato into small dice. Cut the carrot into sticks, about 2.5 cm/1 inch long and cut the leek into rings.

3 Place the cannellini beans and their liquid in a large saucepan. Add the aubergine (eggplant), tomatoes, potatoes, carrot and leek, stirring to mix.

4 Add the stock to the pan and bring to the boil. Reduce the heat and leave to simmer for 15 minutes.

5 Add the basil, dried mushrooms and their soaking liquid and the vermicelli

and simmer for 5 minutes or until all of the vegetables are tender.

6 Remove the pan from the heat and stir in the pesto.

7 Serve with freshly grated Parmesan cheese, if using.

Chickpea (Garbanzo Bean) Soup

A thick vegetable soup which is a delicious meal in itself. Serve with Parmesan cheese and warm sun-dried tomato-flavoured ciabatta bread.

NUTRITIONAL INFORMATION

Calories 297	Sugars 0g	
Protein 11g	Fat 18g	
Carbohydrate ...24g	Saturates 2g	

 5 MINS   15 MINS

SERVES 4

INGREDIENTS

2 tbsp olive oil

2 leeks, sliced

2 courgettes (zucchini), diced

2 garlic cloves, crushed

2 x 400 g/14 oz cans chopped tomatoes

1 tbsp tomato purée (paste)

1 fresh bay leaf

850 ml/1 ½ pints/3 ¾ cups chicken stock

400 g/14 oz can chickpeas (garbanzo beans), drained and rinsed

225 g/8 oz spinach

salt and pepper

TO SERVE

Parmesan cheese

sun-dried tomato bread

COOK'S TIP

Chickpeas (garbanzo beans) are used extensively in North African cuisine and are also found in Italian, Spanish, Middle Eastern and Indian cooking. They have a deliciously nutty flavour with a firm texture and are an excellent canned product.

1 Heat the oil in a large saucepan, add the leeks and courgettes (zucchini) and cook briskly for 5 minutes, stirring constantly.

2 Add the garlic, tomatoes, tomato purée (paste), bay leaf, stock and chickpeas (garbanzo beans). Bring to the boil and simmer for 5 minutes.

3 Shred the spinach finely, add to the soup and cook for 2 minutes. Season.

4 Remove the bay leaf from the soup and discard.

5 Serve the soup with freshly grated Parmesan cheese and sun-dried tomato bread.

Creamy Tomato Soup

This quick and easy creamy soup has a lovely fresh tomato flavour. Basil leaves complement tomatoes perfectly.

NUTRITIONAL INFORMATION

Calories	.218	Sugars	.10g
Protein	.3g	Fat	.19g
Carbohydrate	.10g	Saturates	.11g

5 MINS   25–30 MINS

SERVES 4

I N G R E D I E N T S

50 g/1 ¾ oz/3 tbsp butter

700 g/1 lb 9 oz ripe tomatoes, preferably
plum, roughly chopped

850 ml/1 ½ pints/3 ¾ hot vegetable stock

50 g/1 ¾ oz/ ¼ cup ground almonds

150 ml/¼ pint/ ⅔ cup milk or single (light)
cream

1 tsp sugar

2 tbsp shredded basil leaves

salt and pepper

1 Melt the butter in a large saucepan. Add the tomatoes and cook for 5 minutes until the skins start to wrinkle. Season to taste with salt and pepper.

2 Add the stock to the pan, bring to the boil, cover and simmer for 10 minutes.

3 Meanwhile, under a preheated grill (broiler), lightly toast the ground almonds until they are golden-brown. This will take only 1-2 minutes, so watch them closely.

4 Remove the soup from the heat and place in a food processor and blend the mixture to form a smooth consistency. Alternatively, mash the soup with a potato masher until smooth.

5 Pass the soup through a sieve to remove any tomato skin or pips.

6 Place the soup in the pan and return to the heat. Stir in the milk or cream, toasted ground almonds and sugar. Warm the soup through and add the shredded basil leaves just before serving.

7 Transfer the creamy tomato soup to warm soup bowls and serve hot.

COOK'S TIP

Very fine breadcrumbs can be used instead of the ground almonds, if you prefer. Toast them in the same way as the almonds and add with the milk or cream in step 6.

Calabrian Mushroom Soup

The Calabrian Mountains in southern Italy provide large amounts of wild mushrooms that are rich in flavour and colour.

NUTRITIONAL INFORMATION

Calories 452	Sugars 5g	
Protein 15g	Fat 26g	
Carbohydrate ...42g	Saturates 12g	

 5 MINS 25–30 MINS

SERVES 4

I N G R E D I E N T S

2 tbsp olive oil

1 onion, chopped

450g/1 lb mixed mushrooms, such as ceps, oyster and button

300 ml/ ½ pint/1 ¼ cup milk

850 ml/1 ½ pints/3 ¾ cups hot vegetable stock

8 slices of rustic bread or French stick

2 garlic cloves, crushed

50 g/1 ¾ oz/3 tbsp butter, melted

75 g/2 ¾ oz Gruyère cheese, finely grated

salt and pepper

1 Heat the oil in a large frying pan (skillet) and cook the onion for 3–4 minutes or until soft and golden.

2 Wipe each mushroom with a damp cloth and cut any large mushrooms into smaller, bite-size pieces.

3 Add the mushrooms to the pan, stirring quickly to coat them in the oil.

4 Add the milk to the pan, bring to the boil, cover and leave to simmer for about 5 minutes. Gradually stir in the hot vegetable stock and season with salt and pepper to taste.

5 Under a preheated grill (broiler), toast the bread on both sides until golden.

6 Mix together the garlic and butter and spoon generously over the toast.

7 Place the toast in the bottom of a large tureen or divide it among 4 individual serving bowls and pour over the hot soup. Top with the grated Gruyère cheese and serve at once.

COOK'S TIP

Mushrooms absorb liquid, which can lessen the flavour and affect cooking properties. Therefore, carefully wipe them with a damp cloth rather than rinsing them in water.

Green Soup

This fresh-tasting soup with green (dwarf) beans, cucumber and watercress can be served warm, or chilled on a hot summer day.

NUTRITIONAL INFORMATION

Calories 121	Sugars 2g	
Protein 2g	Fat 8g	
Carbohydrate . . .10g	Saturates 1g	

  5 MINS   25–30 MINS

SERVES 4

INGREDIENTS

1 tbsp olive oil

1 onion, chopped

1 garlic clove, chopped

200 g/7 oz potato, peeled and cut into 2.5 cm/1 inch cubes

700 ml/1 ¼ pints/scant 3 cups vegetable or chicken stock

1 small cucumber or ½ large cucumber, cut into chunks

80 g/3 oz bunch watercress

125 g/4 ½ oz green (dwarf) beans, trimmed and halved lengthwise

salt and pepper

1 Heat the oil in a large pan and fry the onion and garlic for 3–4 minutes or until softened.

2 Add the cubed potato and fry for a further 2–3 minutes.

3 Stir in the stock, bring to the boil and leave to simmer for 5 minutes.

4 Add the cucumber to the pan and cook for a further 3 minutes or until the potatoes are tender. Test by inserting the tip of a knife into the potato cubes – it should pass through easily.

5 Add the watercress and allow to wilt. Then place the soup in a food processor and blend until smooth. Alternatively, before adding the watercress, mash the soup with a potato masher and push through a sieve, then chop the watercress finely and stir into the soup.

6 Bring a small pan of water to the boil and steam the beans for 3–4 minutes or until tender.

7 Add the beans to the soup, season and warm through.

VARIATION

Try using 125 g/4 ½ oz mange tout (snow peas) instead of the beans, if you prefer.

Artichoke Soup

This refreshing chilled soup is ideal for *al fresco* dining. Bear in mind that this soup needs to be chilled for 3-4 hours, so allow plenty of time.

NUTRITIONAL INFORMATION

Calories . . . . . . .159 Sugars 2g
Protein . . . . .2g Fat 15
Carbohydrate . . . .5g Saturates 6g

 5 MINS   15 MINS

SERVES 4

INGREDIENTS

1 tbsp olive oil

1 onion, chopped

1 garlic clove, crushed

2 x 400 g/14 oz can artichoke hearts, drained

600 ml/1 pint/2 ½ cups hot vegetable stock

150 ml/¼ pint/⅔ cup single (light) cream

2 tbsp fresh thyme, stalks removed

2 sun-dried tomatoes, cut into strips

fresh, crusty bread, to serve

1 Heat the oil in a large saucepan and fry the chopped onion and crushed garlic, stirring, for 2-3 minutes or until just softened.

2 Using a sharp knife, roughly chop the artichoke hearts. Add the artichoke pieces to the onion and garlic mixture in the pan. Pour in the hot vegetable stock, stirring well.

3 Bring the mixture to the boil, then reduce the heat and leave to simmer, covered, for about 3 minutes.

4 Place the mixture into a food processor and blend until smooth. Alternatively, push the mixture through a sieve to remove any lumps.

5 Return the soup to the saucepan. Stir the single (light) cream and fresh thyme into the soup.

6 Transfer the soup to a large bowl, cover, and leave to chill in the refrigerator for about 3-4 hours.

7 Transfer the chilled soup to individual soup bowls and garnish with strips of sun-dried tomato. Serve with crusty bread.

VARIATION

Try adding 2 tablespoons of dry vermouth, such as Martini, to the soup in step 5, if you wish.

Red (Bell) Pepper Soup

This soup has a real Mediterranean flavour, using sweet red (bell) peppers, tomato, chilli and basil. It is great served with a warm olive bread.

NUTRITIONAL INFORMATION

Calories	55	Sugar	.........10g
Protein	.........2g	Fats	.........0.5g
Carbohydrates	...11g	Saturates	.....0.1g

 5 MINS   25 MINS

SERVES 4

INGREDIENTS

225 g/8 oz red (bell) peppers, seeded and sliced

1 onion, sliced

2 garlic cloves, crushed

1 green chilli, chopped

300 ml/½ pint/1½ cups passata (sieved tomatoes)

600 ml/1 pint/2½ cups vegetable stock

2 tbsp chopped basil

fresh basil sprigs, to garnish

1 Put the (bell) peppers in a large saucepan with the onion, garlic and chilli. Add the passata (sieved tomatoes) and vegetable stock and bring to the boil, stirring well.

2 Reduce the heat to a simmer and cook for 20 minutes or until the (bell) peppers have softened. Drain, reserving the liquid and vegetables separately.

3 Sieve the vegetables by pressing through a sieve (strainer) with the back of a spoon. Alternatively, blend in a food processor until smooth.

4 Return the vegetable purée to a clean saucepan with the reserved cooking liquid. Add the basil and heat through until hot. Garnish the soup with fresh basil sprigs and serve.

VARIATION

This soup is also delicious served cold with 150 ml/¼ pint/¼ cup of natural (unsweetened) yogurt swirled into it.

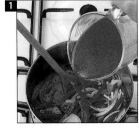

Yogurt & Spinach Soup

Whole young spinach leaves add vibrant colour to this unusual soup.
Serve with hot, crusty bread for a nutritious light meal.

NUTRITIONAL INFORMATION

Calories	227	Sugars	........13g
Protein	........14g	Fat	..........7g
Carbohydrate	...29g	Saturates	......2g

 15 MINS 30 MINS

SERVES 4

I N G R E D I E N T S

600 ml/1 pint/2½ cups chicken stock

60 g/2 oz/4 tbsp long-grain rice, rinsed and drained

4 tbsp water

1 tbsp cornflour (cornstarch)

600 ml/1 pint/2½ cups low-fat natural yogurt

juice of 1 lemon

3 egg yolks, lightly beaten

350 g/12 oz young spinach leaves, washed and drained

salt and pepper

1 Pour the stock into a large pan, season and bring to the boil. Add the rice and simmer for 10 minutes, until barely cooked. Remove from the heat.

2 Combine the water and cornflour (cornstarch) to make a smooth paste.

3 Pour the yogurt into a second pan and stir in the cornflour (cornstarch) mixture. Set the pan over a low heat and bring the yogurt slowly to the boil, stirring with a wooden spoon in one direction only. This will stabilize the yogurt and prevent it from separating or curdling on contact with the hot stock. When the yogurt has reached boiling point, stand the pan on a heat diffuser and leave to simmer slowly for 10 minutes. Remove the pan from the heat and allow the mixture to cool slightly before stirring in the beaten egg yolks.

4 Pour the yogurt mixture into the stock, stir in the lemon juice and stir to blend thoroughly. Keep the soup warm, but do not allow it to boil.

5 Blanch the washed and drained spinach leaves in a large pan of boiling, salted water for 2-3 minutes until they begin to soften but have not wilted. Tip the spinach into a colander, drain well and stir it into the soup. Let the spinach warm through. Taste the soup and adjust the seasoning if necessary. Serve in wide shallow soup plates, with hot, fresh crusty bread.

Mushroom & Ginger Soup

Thai soups are very quickly and easily put together, and are cooked so that each ingredient can still be tasted in the finished dish.

NUTRITIONAL INFORMATION

Calories	74	Sugars	.........1g
Protein	.........3g	Fat	..........3g
Carbohydrate	....9g	Saturates	.....0.4g

1½ HOURS   15 MINS

SERVES 4

I N G R E D I E N T S

15 g/½ oz/¼ cup dried Chinese mushrooms or 125 g/4½ oz/1⅓ cups field or chestnut (crimini) mushrooms

1 litre/1¾ pints/4 cups hot fresh vegetable stock

125 g/4½ oz thread egg noodles

2 tsp sunflower oil

3 garlic cloves, crushed

2.5 cm/1 inch piece ginger, shredded finely

½ tsp mushroom ketchup

1 tsp light soy sauce

125 g/4½ oz/2 cups bean sprouts

coriander (cilantro) leaves, to garnish

1 Soak the dried Chinese mushrooms (if using) for at least 30 minutes in 300 ml/½ pint/1¼ cups of the hot vegetable stock. Remove the stalks and discard, then slice the mushrooms. Reserve the stock.

2 Cook the noodles for 2–3 minutes in boiling water. Drain and rinse. Set them aside.

3 Heat the oil over a high heat in a wok or large, heavy frying pan (skillet). Add the garlic and ginger, stir and add the mushrooms. Stir over a high heat for 2 minutes.

4 Add the remaining vegetable stock with the reserved stock and bring to the boil. Add the mushroom ketchup and soy sauce.

5 Stir in the bean sprouts and cook until tender. Put some noodles in each bowl and ladle the soup on top. Garnish with coriander (cilantro) leaves and serve immediately.

COOK'S TIP

Rice noodles contain no fat and are ideal for for anyone on a low-fat diet.

Tomato & (Bell) Pepper Soup

Sweet red (bell) peppers and tangy tomatoes are blended together in a smooth vegetable soup that makes a perfect starter or light lunch.

NUTRITIONAL INFORMATION

Calories	52	Sugars	........9g
Protein	.........3g	Fat	..........0.4g
Carbohydrate	...10g	Saturates	......0g

    1¼ HOURS   35 MINS

SERVES 4

INGREDIENTS

2 large red (bell) peppers

1 large onion, chopped

2 sticks celery, trimmed and chopped

1 garlic clove, crushed

600 ml/1 pint/2½ cups fresh vegetable stock

2 bay leaves

2 x 400 g/14 oz cans plum tomatoes

salt and pepper

2 spring onions (scallions), finely shredded, to garnish

crusty bread, to serve

1 Preheat the grill (broiler) to hot. Halve and deseed the (bell) peppers, arrange them on the grill (broiler) rack and cook, turning occasionally, for 8–10 minutes until softened and charred.

2 Leave to cool slightly, then carefully peel off the charred skin. Reserving a small piece for garnish, chop the (bell) pepper flesh and place in a large saucepan.

3 Mix in the onion, celery and garlic. Add the stock and the bay leaves. Bring to the boil, cover and simmer for 15 minutes. Remove from the heat.

4 Stir in the tomatoes and transfer to a blender. Process for a few seconds until smooth. Return to the saucepan.

5 Season to taste and heat for 3–4 minutes until piping hot. Ladle into warm bowls and garnish with the reserved (bell) pepper cut into strips and the spring onion (scallion). Serve with crusty bread.

COOK'S TIP

If you prefer a coarser, more robust soup, lightly mash the tomatoes with a wooden spoon and omit the blending process in step 4.

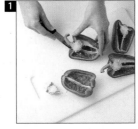

Carrot, Apple & Celery Soup

For this fresh-tasting soup, use your favourite eating (dessert) apple rather than a cooking variety, which will give too tart a flavour.

NUTRITIONAL INFORMATION

Calories 153g	Sugars 34g	
Protein 2g	Fat 1g	
Carbohydrate . . .36g	Saturates 0.2g	

1¼ HOURS   40 MINS

SERVES 4

INGREDIENTS

900 g/2 lb carrots, finely diced

1 medium onion, chopped

3 sticks celery, trimmed and diced

1 litre/1¾ pints/1 quart fresh vegetable stock

3 medium-sized eating (dessert) apples

2 tbsp tomato purée (paste)

1 bay leaf

2 tsp caster (superfine) sugar

¼ large lemon

salt and pepper

celery leaves, washed and shredded, to garnish

1 Place the prepared carrots, onion and celery in a large saucepan and add the stock. Bring to the boil, cover and simmer for 10 minutes.

2 Meanwhile, peel, core and dice 2 of the apples. Add the pieces of apple, tomato purée (paste), bay leaf and caster (superfine) sugar to the saucepan and bring to the boil. Reduce the heat, half cover and allow to simmer for 20 minutes. Remove and discard the bay leaf.

3 Meanwhile, wash, core and cut the remaining apple into thin slices, leaving on the skin.

4 Place the apple slices in a small saucepan and squeeze over the lemon juice. Heat the apple slices gently and simmer for 1–2 minutes until tender.

5 Drain the apple slices and set aside until required.

6 Place the carrot and apple mixture in a blender or food processor and blend until smooth. Alternatively, press the mixture through a sieve (strainer) with the back of a wooden spoon.

7 Gently re-heat the soup if necessary and season with salt and pepper to taste. Serve the soup topped with the reserved apple slices and shredded celery leaves.

 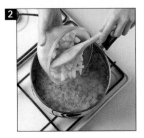 

Spiced Cauliflower Soup

A thick puréed soup flavoured with Indian spices and yogurt. Serve with hot naan bread.

NUTRITIONAL INFORMATION

Calories	123	Sugars	........13g
Protein	.........8g	Fat	..........4g
Carbohydrate	...14g	Saturates	......1g

10 MINS   25 MINS

SERVES 4

INGREDIENTS

350 g/12 oz cauliflower, divided into small florets

350 g/12 oz swede (rutabaga), diced

1 onion, chopped

1 tbsp oil

3 tbsp water

1 garlic clove, crushed

2 tsp grated ginger root

1 tsp cumin seeds

1 tsp black mustard seeds

2 tsp ground coriander

2 tsp ground turmeric

850 ml/1½ pints/3½ cups hot vegetable stock

300 ml/½ pint/1¼ cups low-fat yogurt

salt and pepper

chopped fresh coriander (cilantro), to garnish

1 Place the cauliflower, swede (rutabaga), onion, oil and water in a large bowl. Cover and microwave on HIGH power for 10 minutes, stirring halfway through.

2 Add the garlic, ginger and spices. Stir well, cover and cook in the microwave on HIGH power for 2 minutes.

3 Pour in the stock, cover and microwave on HIGH power for 10 minutes. Leave to stand, covered, for 5 minutes.

4 Strain the vegetables and reserve the liquid. Purée the vegetables with a little of the reserved liquid in a food processor or blender, until smooth and creamy. Alternatively, either mash the soup or press it through a sieve (strainer).

5 Pour the vegetable purée and remaining reserved liquid into a clean bowl and mix well. Season to taste.

6 Stir in the yogurt and cook on HIGH power for 3–4 minutes until hot but not boiling, otherwise the yogurt will curdle. Ladle into warmed bowls and serve garnished with chopped fresh coriander (cilantro).

Pumpkin Soup

This is an American classic that has now become popular worldwide. When pumpkin is out of season use butternut squash in its place.

NUTRITIONAL INFORMATION

Calories 112	Sugars 7g	
Protein 4g	Fat 7g	
Carbohydrate 8g	Saturates 2g	

 10 MINS   30 MINS

SERVES 6

I N G R E D I E N T S

about 1 kg/2 lb 4 oz pumpkin

40 g/1½ oz/3 tbsp butter or margarine

1 onion, sliced thinly

1 garlic clove, crushed

900 ml/1½ pints/3½ cups vegetable stock

½ tsp ground ginger

1 tbsp lemon juice

3–4 thinly pared strips of orange

  rind (optional)

1–2 bay leaves or 1 bouquet garni

300 ml/½ pint/1¼ cups milk

salt and pepper

TO GARNISH

4–6 tablespoons single (light) or double

  (heavy) cream, natural yogurt

  or fromage frais

snipped chives

1 Peel the pumpkin, remove the seeds and then cut the flesh into 2.5 cm/1 inch cubes.

2 Melt the butter or margarine in a large, heavy-based saucepan. Add the onion and garlic and fry over a low heat until soft but not coloured.

3 Add the pumpkin and toss with the onion for 2–3 minutes.

4 Add the stock and bring to the boil over a medium heat. Season to taste with salt and pepper and add the ginger, lemon juice, strips of orange rind, if using, and bay leaves or bouquet garni. Cover and simmer over a low heat for about 20 minutes, until the pumpkin is tender.

5 Discard the orange rind, if using, and the bay leaves or bouquet garni. Cool the soup slightly, then press through a strainer or process in a food processor until smooth. Pour into a clean saucepan.

6 Add the milk and reheat gently. Adjust the seasoning. Garnish with a swirl of cream, natural yogurt or fromage frais and snipped chives, and serve.

Chinese Potato & Pork Broth

In this recipe the pork is seasoned with traditional Chinese flavourings – soy sauce, rice wine vinegar and a dash of sesame oil.

NUTRITIONAL INFORMATION

Calories 166   Sugars 2g
Protein ....10g   Fat 5g
Carbohydrate ...26g   Saturates 1g

 5 MINS   20 MINS

SERVES 4

I N G R E D I E N T S

1 litre/1¾ pints/4½ cups chicken stock

2 large potatoes, diced

2 tbsp rice wine vinegar

2 tbsp cornflour (cornstarch)

4 tbsp water

125 g/4½ oz pork fillet, sliced

1 tbsp light soy sauce

1 tsp sesame oil

1 carrot, cut into very thin strips

1 tsp ginger root, chopped

3 spring onions (scallions), sliced thinly

1 red (bell) pepper, sliced

225 g/8 oz can bamboo shoots, drained

1 Add the chicken stock, diced potatoes and 1 tbsp of the rice wine vinegar to a saucepan and bring to the boil. Reduce the heat until the stock is just simmering.

2 Mix the cornflour (cornstarch) with the water then stir into the hot stock.

3 Bring the stock back to the boil, stirring until thickened, then reduce the heat until it is just simmering again.

4 Place the pork slices in a dish and season with the remaining rice wine vinegar, the soy sauce and sesame oil.

5 Add the pork slices, carrot strips and ginger to the stock and cook for 10 minutes. Stir in the spring onions (scallions), red (bell) pepper and bamboo shoots. Cook for a further 5 minutes. Pour the soup into warmed bowls and serve immediately.

VARIATION

For extra heat, add 1 chopped red chilli or 1 tsp of chilli powder to the soup in step 5.

Chicken, Noodle & Corn Soup

The vermicelli gives this Chinese-style soup an Italian twist, but you can use egg noodles if you prefer.

NUTRITIONAL INFORMATION

Calories 401	Sugars 6g
Protein 31g	Fat 24g
Carbohydrate . . .17g	Saturates 13g

5 MINS   25 MINS

SERVES 4

I N G R E D I E N T S

450 g/1 lb boned chicken breasts,
  cut into strips

1.2 litres/2 pints/5 cups chicken stock

150 ml/¼ pint/⅝ cup double (heavy)
  cream

100 g/3½ oz/¾ cup dried vermicelli

1 tbsp cornflour (cornstarch)

3 tbsp milk

175 g/6 oz sweetcorn (corn-on-the-cob)
  kernels

salt and pepper

finely chopped spring onion (scallions),
  to garnish (optional)

1 Put the chicken strips, chicken stock and double (heavy) cream into a large saucepan and bring to the boil over a low heat.

2 Reduce the heat slightly and simmer for about 20 minutes. Season the soup with salt and black pepper to taste.

3 Meanwhile, cook the vermicelli in lightly salted boiling water for 10-12 minutes, until just tender. Drain the pasta and keep warm.

4 In a small bowl, mix together the cornflour (cornstarch) and milk to make a smooth paste. Stir the cornflour

(cornstarch) paste into the soup until thickened.

5 Add the sweetcorn (corn-on-the-cob) and vermicelli to the pan and heat through.

6 Transfer the soup to a warm tureen or individual soup bowls, garnish with spring onions (scallions), if desired, and serve immediately.

VARIATION

For crab and sweetcorn soup, substitute 450 g/1 lb cooked crabmeat for the chicken breasts. Flake the crabmeat well before adding it to the saucepan and reduce the cooking time by 10 minutes.

Chicken & Bean Soup

This hearty and nourishing soup, combining chickpeas (garbanzo beans) and chicken, is an ideal starter for a family supper.

NUTRITIONAL INFORMATION

Calories 347	Sugars 2g
Protein 28g	Fat 11g
Carbohydrate . . .37g	Saturates 4g

5 MINS   1¾ HOURS

SERVES 4

INGREDIENTS

25 g/1 oz/2 tbsp butter

3 spring onions (scallions), chopped

2 garlic cloves, crushed

1 fresh marjoram sprig, finely chopped

350 g/12 oz boned chicken breasts, diced

1.2 litres/2 pints/5 cups chicken stock

350 g/12 oz can chickpeas (garbanzo beans), drained

1 bouquet garni

1 red (bell) pepper, diced

1 green (bell) pepper, diced

115 g/4 oz/1 cup small dried pasta shapes, such as elbow macaroni

salt and white pepper

croûtons, to serve

COOK'S TIP

If you prefer, you can use dried chickpeas (garbanzo beans). Cover with cold water and set aside to soak for 5–8 hours. Drain and add the beans to the soup, according to the recipe, and allow an additional 30 minutes– 1 hour cooking time.

1 Melt the butter in a large saucepan. Add the spring onions (scallions), garlic, sprig of fresh marjoram and the diced chicken and cook, stirring frequently, over a medium heat for 5 minutes.

2 Add the chicken stock, chickpeas (garbanzo beans) and bouquet garni and season with salt and white pepper.

3 Bring the soup to the boil, lower the heat and simmer for about 2 hours.

4 Add the diced (bell) peppers and pasta to the pan, then simmer for a further 20 minutes.

5 Transfer the soup to a warm tureen. To serve, ladle the soup into individual serving bowls and serve immediately, garnished with the croûtons.

Peking Duck Soup

This is a hearty and robustly flavoured soup, containing pieces of duck and vegetables cooked in a rich stock.

NUTRITIONAL INFORMATION

Calories 92	Sugars 3g	
Protein 8g	Fat 5g	
Carbohydrate 3g	Saturates 1g	

  5 MINS   35 MINS

SERVES 4

INGREDIENTS

125 g/4½ oz lean duck breast meat

225 g/8 oz Chinese leaves
   (cabbage)

850 ml/1½ pints/3¾ cups chicken or
   duck stock

1 tbsp dry sherry or rice wine

1 tbsp light soy sauce

2 garlic cloves, crushed

pinch of ground star anise

1 tbsp sesame seeds

1 tsp sesame oil

1 tbsp chopped fresh parsley

1 Remove the skin from the duck breast and finely dice the flesh.

2 Using a sharp knife, shred the Chinese leaves (cabbage).

3 Put the stock in a large saucepan and bring to the boil. Add the sherry or rice wine, soy sauce, diced duck meat and shredded Chinese leaves and stir to mix thoroughly. Reduce the heat and leave to simmer gently for 15 minutes.

4 Stir in the garlic and star anise and cook over a low heat for a further 10–15 minutes, or until the duck is tender.

5 Meanwhile, dry-fry the sesame seeds in a preheated, heavy-based frying pan (skillet) or wok, stirring constantly.

6 Remove the sesame seeds from the pan and stir them into the soup, together with the sesame oil and chopped fresh parsley.

7 Spoon the soup into warm bowls and serve immediately.

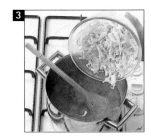

VARIATION

If Chinese leaves (cabbage) are unavailable, use leafy green cabbage instead. You may wish to adjust the quantity to taste, as Western cabbage has a stronger flavour and odour than Chinese leaves (cabbage).

Chunky Potato & Beef Soup

This is a real winter warmer – pieces of tender beef and chunky mixed vegetables are cooked in a liquor flavoured with sherry.

NUTRITIONAL INFORMATION

Calories	187	Sugars 3g
Protein	. . . . .14g	Fat 9g
Carbohydrate	. . .12g	Saturates 2g

 5 MINS   35 MINS

SERVES 4

INGREDIENTS

2 tbsp vegetable oil

225 g/8 oz lean braising or frying steak, cut into strips

225 g/8 oz new potatoes, halved

1 carrot, diced

2 celery sticks, sliced

2 leeks, sliced

850 ml/1½ pints/3¾ cups beef stock

8 baby sweetcorn cobs, sliced

1 bouquet garni

2 tbsp dry sherry

salt and pepper

chopped fresh parsley, to garnish

1 Heat the vegetable oil in a large saucepan.

2 Add the strips of meat to the saucepan and cook for 3 minutes, turning constantly.

3 Add the halved potatoes, diced carrot and sliced celery and leeks. Cook for a further 5 minutes, stirring.

4 Pour the beef stock into the saucepan and bring to the boil. Reduce the heat until the liquid is simmering, then add the sliced baby sweetcorn cobs and the bouquet garni.

5 Cook the soup for a further 20 minutes or until cooked through.

6 Remove the bouquet garni from the saucepan and discard. Stir the dry sherry into the soup and then season to taste with salt and pepper.

7 Pour the soup into warmed bowls and garnish with the chopped fresh parsley. Serve at once with crusty bread.

COOK'S TIP

Make double the quantity of soup and freeze the remainder in a rigid container for later use. When ready to use, leave in the refrigerator to defrost thoroughly, then heat until piping hot.

Chicken & Leek Soup

This satisfying soup can be served as a main course. You can add rice and (bell) peppers to make it even more hearty, as well as colourful.

NUTRITIONAL INFORMATION

Calories	183	Sugar	........4g
Protein	........21g	Fats	..........9g
Carbohydrates	....4g	Saturates	......5g

 5 MINS 1¼ HOURS

SERVES 4–6

I N G R E D I E N T S

25 g/1 oz/2 tbsp butter

350 g/12 oz boneless chicken

350 g/12 oz leeks, cut into 2.5-cm/
   1-inch pieces

1.2 litres/2 pints/5 cups chicken stock

1 bouquet garni sachet

8 pitted prunes, halved

salt and white pepper

cooked rice and diced (bell) peppers
   (optional)

1 Melt the butter in a large saucepan.

2 Add the chicken and leeks to the saucepan and fry for 8 minutes.

3 Add the chicken stock and bouquet garni sachet and stir well.

4 Season well with salt and pepper to taste.

5 Bring the soup to the boil and simmer for 45 minutes.

6 Add the prunes to the saucepan with some cooked rice and diced (bell) peppers (if using) and simmer for about 20 minutes.

7 Remove the bouquet garni sachet from the soup and discard. Serve the chicken and leek soup immediately.

VARIATION

Instead of the bouquet garni sachet, you can use a bunch of fresh mixed herbs, tied together with string. Choose herbs such as parsley, thyme and rosemary.

Chicken & Pasta Broth

This satisfying soup makes a good lunch or supper dish and you can use any vegetables you like. Children will love the tiny pasta shapes.

NUTRITIONAL INFORMATION

Calories	185	Sugars	.........5g
Protein	........17g	Fat	...........5g
Carbohydrate	...20g	Saturates	.......1g

🍲 5 MINS   🕐 15–20 MINS

SERVES 6

I N G R E D I E N T S

350 g/12 oz boneless chicken breasts

2 tbsp sunflower oil

1 medium onion, diced

250 g/9 oz/1 ½ cups carrots, diced

250 g/9 oz cauliflower florets

850 ml/1 ½ pints/3 ¾ cups chicken stock

2 tsp dried mixed herbs

125 g/4 ½ oz small pasta shapes

salt and pepper

Parmesan cheese (optional) and crusty
  bread, to serve

1 Using a sharp knife, finely dice the chicken, discarding any skin.

2 Heat the oil in a large saucepan and quickly sauté the chicken, onion, carrots and cauliflower until they are lightly coloured.

3 Stir in the chicken stock and dried mixed herbs and bring to the boil.

4 Add the pasta shapes to the pan and return to the boil. Cover the pan and leave the broth to simmer for 10 minutes, stirring occasionally to prevent the pasta shapes from sticking together.

5 Season the broth with salt and pepper to taste and sprinkle with Parmesan cheese, if using. Serve the broth with fresh crusty bread.

COOK'S TIP

You can use any small pasta shapes for this soup – try conchigliette or ditalini or even spaghetti broken up into small pieces. To make a fun soup for children you could add animal-shaped or alphabet pasta.

Chicken & Sweetcorn Soup

A quick and satisfying soup, full of delicious flavours and many different textures.

NUTRITIONAL INFORMATION

Calories 200	Sugars 6g	
Protein 10g	Fat 12g	
Carbohydrate ...13g	Saturates 5g	

 10 MINS   40 MINS

SERVES 2

I N G R E D I E N T S

2 tsp oil

15 g/½ oz/¼ cup butter or margarine

1 small onion, chopped finely

1 chicken leg quarter or 2–3 drumsticks

1 tbsp plain (all-purpose) flour

600 ml/1 pint/2½ cups chicken stock

½ small red, yellow or orange (bell) pepper, seeded and chopped finely

2 large tomatoes, peeled and chopped

2 tsp tomato purée (paste)

200 g/7 oz can of sweetcorn, drained

generous pinch of dried oregano

¼ tsp ground coriander

salt and pepper

chopped fresh parsley, to garnish

1 Heat the oil and butter or margarine in a saucepan and fry the onion until beginning to soften. Cut the chicken quarter (if using) into 2 pieces. Add the chicken and fry until golden brown.

2 Add the flour and cook for 1–2 minutes. Then add the stock, bring to the boil and simmer for 5 minutes.

3 Add the (bell) pepper, tomatoes, tomato purée (paste), sweetcorn, oregano, coriander and seasoning. Cover and simmer gently for about 20 minutes until the chicken is very tender.

4 Remove the chicken from the soup, strip off the flesh and chop finely. Return the chopped meat to the soup.

5 Adjust the seasoning and simmer for a further 2–3 minutes before sprinkling with parsley and serving very hot with crusty bread.

COOK'S TIP

If preferred, the chicken may be removed from the soup when tender to serve separately.

Spicy Chicken Noodle Soup

This filling soup is filled with spicy flavours and bright colours for a really attractive and hearty dish.

NUTRITIONAL INFORMATION

Calories	286	Sugars	.......21g
Protein	........22g	Fat	...........6g
Carbohydrate	...37g	Saturates	.......1g

 15 MINS   20 MINS

SERVES 4

INGREDIENTS

2 tbsp tamarind paste

4 red chillies, finely chopped

2 cloves garlic, crushed

2.5 cm/1-inch piece Thai ginger, peeled and very finely chopped

4 tbsp fish sauce

2 tbsp palm sugar or caster (superfine) sugar

8 lime leaves, roughly torn

1.2 litres/2 pints/5 cups chicken stock

350 g/12 oz boneless chicken breast

100 g/3½ oz carrots, very thinly sliced

350 g/12 oz sweet potato, diced

100 g/3½ oz baby corn cobs, halved

3 tbsp fresh coriander (cilantro), roughly chopped

100 g/3½ oz cherry tomatoes, halved

150 g/5½ oz flat rice noodles

fresh coriander (cilantro), chopped, to garnish

1 Preheat a large wok or frying pan (skillet). Place the tamarind paste, chillies, garlic, ginger, fish sauce, sugar, lime leaves and chicken stock in the wok and bring to the boil, stirring constantly. Reduce the heat and cook for about 5 minutes.

2 Using a sharp knife, thinly slice the chicken. Add the chicken to the wok and cook for a further 5 minutes, stirring the mixture well.

3 Reduce the heat and add the carrots, sweet potato and baby corn cobs to the wok. Leave to simmer, uncovered, for 5 minutes, or until the vegetables are just tender and the chicken is completely cooked through.

4 Stir in the chopped fresh coriander (cilantro), cherry tomatoes and flat rice noodles.

5 Leave the soup to simmer for about 5 minutes, or until the noodles are tender.

6 Garnish the spicy chicken noodle soup with chopped fresh coriander (cilantro) and serve hot.

Pork & Szechuan Vegetable

Sold in cans, Szechuan preserved vegetable is pickled mustard root which is quite hot and salty, so rinse in water before use.

NUTRITIONAL INFORMATION

Calories	135	Sugars	.........1g
Protein	........14g	Fat	..........7g
Carbohydrate	....3g	Saturates	.......2g

 5 MINS 5 MINS

SERVES 4

I N G R E D I E N T S

250 g/9 oz pork fillet

2 tsp cornflour (cornstarch) paste

125 g/4½ oz Szechuan preserved vegetable

700 ml/1¼ pints/3 cups Chinese stock or water

salt and pepper

a few drops sesame oil (optional)

2-3 spring onions (scallions), sliced, to garnish

1 Preheat a wok or large, heavy-based frying pan (skillet).

2 Using a sharp knife, cut the pork across the grain into thin shreds.

3 Mix the pork with the cornflour (cornstarch) paste until the pork is completely coated in the mixture.

4 Thoroughly wash and rinse the Szechuan preserved vegetable, then pat dry on absorbent kitchen paper (paper towels). Cut the Szechuan preserved vegetable into thin shreds the same size as the pork.

5 Pour the Chinese stock or water into the wok or frying pan (skillet) and bring to a rolling boil. Add the pork to the wok and stir to separate the shreds. Return to the boil.

6 Add the shredded Szechuan preserved vegetable and bring back to the boil once more.

7 Adjust the seasoning to taste and sprinkle with sesame oil. Serve hot, garnished with spring onions (scallions).

COOK'S TIP

Szechuan preserved vegetable is actually mustard green root, pickled in salt and chillies. Available in cans from specialist Chinese supermarkets, it gives a crunchy, spicy taste to dishes. Rinse in cold water before use and store in the refrigerator.

Lemon & Chicken Soup

This delicately flavoured summer soup is surprisingly easy to make, and tastes delicious.

NUTRITIONAL INFORMATION

Calories 506	Sugars 4g
Protein 19g	Fat 31g
Carbohydrate . . .41g	Saturates 19g

  5-10 MINS   1¼ HOURS

SERVES 4

INGREDIENTS

60 g/2 oz/4 tbsp butter

8 shallots, thinly sliced

2 carrots, thinly sliced

2 celery sticks (stalks), thinly sliced

225 g/8 oz boned chicken breasts,
  finely chopped

3 lemons

1.2 litres/2 pints/5 cups chicken stock

225 g/8 oz dried spaghetti, broken into
  small pieces

150 ml/¼ pint/⅝ cup double (heavy) cream

salt and white pepper

TO GARNISH

fresh parsley sprig

3 lemon slices, halved

COOK'S TIP

You can prepare this soup up to the end of step 3 in advance, so that all you need do before serving is heat it through before adding the pasta and the finishing touches.

1 Melt the butter in a large saucepan. Add the shallots, carrots, celery and chicken and cook over a low heat, stirring occasionally, for 8 minutes.

2 Thinly pare the lemons and blanch the lemon rind in boiling water for 3 minutes. Squeeze the juice from the lemons.

3 Add the lemon rind and juice to the pan, together with the chicken stock. Bring slowly to the boil over a low heat

and simmer for 40 minutes, stirring occasionally.

4 Add the spaghetti to the pan and cook for 15 minutes. Season to taste with salt and white pepper and add the cream. Heat through, but do not allow the soup to boil or it will curdle.

5 Pour the soup into a tureen or individual bowls, garnish with the parsley and half slices of lemon and serve immediately.

Beef Soup with Rice

Strips of tender lean beef are combined with crisp water chestnuts and cooked rice in a tasty beef broth with a tang of orange.

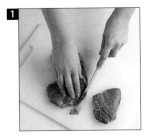

NUTRITIONAL INFORMATION

Calories . . . . .210 Sugar 4g
Protein . . . . .20g Fats 5g
Carbohydrates . . .21g Saturates 2g

 25 MINS   25 MINS

SERVES 4

INGREDIENTS

350 g/12 oz lean beef (such as rump or sirloin)

1 litre/1¾ pints/1 quart beef stock

1 cinnamon stick, broken

2 star anise

2 tbsp dark soy sauce

2 tbsp dry sherry

3 tbsp tomato purée (paste)

115 g/4 oz can water chestnuts, drained and sliced

175 g/6 oz/3 cups cooked white rice

1 tsp zested orange rind

6 tbsp orange juice

salt and pepper

TO GARNISH

strips of orange rind

2 tbsp chives, snipped

1 Carefully trim away any fat from the beef. Cut the beef into thin strips and then place into a large saucepan.

2 Pour over the stock and add the cinnamon, star anise, soy sauce, sherry, tomato purée (paste) and water chestnuts. Bring to the boil, skimming away any surface scum with a flat ladle. Cover the pan and simmer gently for about 20 minutes.

3 Skim the soup with a flat ladle to remove any more scum. Remove and discard the cinnamon and star anise and blot the surface with absorbent kitchen paper to remove any fat.

4 Stir in the rice, orange rind and juice. Check the seasoning. Heat through for 2–3 minutes before ladling into warm bowls. Serve garnished with strips of orange rind and snipped chives.

COOK'S TIP

Omit the rice for a lighter soup that is an ideal starter for an Oriental meal of many courses. For a more substantial soup that would be a meal in its own right, add diced vegetables such as carrot, (bell) pepper, sweetcorn or courgette (zucchini).

Chicken Wonton Soup

This Chinese-style soup is delicious as a starter to an oriental meal or as a light meal.

NUTRITIONAL INFORMATION

Calories	101	Sugars	......0.3g
Protein	........14g	Fat	..........4g
Carbohydrate	....3g	Saturates	.......1g

 15 MINS 10 MINS

SERVES 4-6

I N G R E D I E N T S

FILLING

350 g/12 oz minced (ground) chicken

1 tbsp soy sauce

1 tsp grated, fresh ginger root

1 garlic clove, crushed

2 tsp sherry

2 spring onions (scallions), chopped

1 tsp sesame oil

1 egg white

½ tsp cornflour (cornstarch)

½ tsp sugar

about 35 wonton wrappers

SOUP

1.5 litres/2¾ pints/6 cups chicken stock

1 tbsp light soy sauce

1 spring onion (scallion), shredded

1 small carrot, cut into very thin slices

1 Place all the ingredients for the filling in a large bowl and mix until thoroughly combined.

2 Place a small spoonful of the filling in the centre of each wonton wrapper.

3 Dampen the edges and gather up the wonton wrapper to form a small pouch enclosing the filling.

4 Cook the filled wontons in boiling water for 1 minute or until they float to the top. Remove with a slotted spoon and set aside.

5 Bring the chicken stock to the boil. Add the soy sauce, spring onion (scallion) and carrot.

6 Add the wontons to the soup and simmer gently for 2 minutes. Serve.

COOK'S TIP

Make double quantities of wonton skins and freeze the remainder. Place small squares of baking parchment in between each skin, then place in a freezer bag and freeze. Defrost thoroughly before using.

Fish Soup

There are many varieties of fish soup in Italy, some including shellfish. This one, from Tuscany, is more like a chowder.

NUTRITIONAL INFORMATION

Calories 305	Sugars 3g	
Protein 47g	Fat 7g	
Carbohydrate 11g	Saturates 1g	

   5–10 MINS   1 HOUR

SERVES 6

I N G R E D I E N T S

1 kg/2 lb 4 oz assorted prepared fish (including mixed fish fillets, squid, etc.)

2 onions, sliced thinly

2 celery stalks, sliced thinly

a few sprigs of parsley

2 bay leaves

150 ml/ ¼ pint/ ⅔ cup white wine

1 litre/1 ¾ pints/4 cups water

2 tbsp olive oil

1 garlic clove, crushed

1 carrot, chopped finely

400 g/14 oz can peeled tomatoes, puréed

2 potatoes, chopped

1 tbsp tomato purée (paste)

1 tsp chopped fresh oregano or ½ tsp dried oregano

350 g/12 oz fresh mussels

175 g/6 oz peeled prawns (shrimp)

2 tbsp chopped fresh parsley

salt and pepper

crusty bread, to serve

1 Cut the fish into slices and put into a pan with half the onion and celery, the parsley, bay leaves, wine and water. Bring to the boil, cover and simmer for 25 minutes.

2 Strain the fish stock and discard the vegetables. Skin the fish, remove any bones and reserve.

3 Heat the oil in a pan. Fry the remaining onion and celery with the garlic and carrot until soft but not coloured, stirring occasionally. Add the puréed canned tomatoes, potatoes, tomato purée (paste), oregano, reserved stock and seasoning. Bring to the boil and simmer for about 15 minutes or until the potato is almost tender.

4 Meanwhile, thoroughly scrub the mussels. Add the mussels to the pan with the prawns (shrimp) and leave to simmer for about 5 minutes or until the mussels have opened (discard any that remain closed).

5 Return the fish to the soup with the chopped parsley, bring back to the boil and simmer for 5 minutes. Adjust the seasoning.

6 Serve the soup in warmed bowls with chunks of fresh crusty bread, or put a toasted slice of crusty bread in the bottom of each bowl before adding the soup. If possible, remove a few half shells from the mussels before serving.

Smoked Haddock Soup

Smoked haddock gives this soup a wonderfully rich flavour, while the mashed potatoes and cream thicken and enrich the stock.

NUTRITIONAL INFORMATION

Calories 169	Sugars 8g	
Protein 16g	Fat 5g	
Carbohydrate . . .16g	Saturates 3g	

🕐 25 MINS 🕐 40 MINS

SERVES 4–6

I N G R E D I E N T S

225 g/8 oz smoked haddock fillet

1 onion, chopped finely

1 garlic clove, crushed

600 ml/1 pint/2½ cups water

600 ml/1 pint/2½ cups skimmed milk

225–350 g/8–12 oz/1–1½ cups hot mashed potatoes

30 g/1 oz/2 tbsp butter

about 1 tbsp lemon juice

6 tbsp low-fat natural fromage frais

4 tbsp fresh parsley, chopped

salt and pepper

1 Put the fish, onion, garlic and water into a saucepan. Bring to the boil, cover and simmer for 15–20 minutes.

2 Remove the fish from the pan, strip off the skin and remove all the bones. Flake the flesh finely.

3 Return the skin and bones to the cooking liquid and simmer for 10 minutes. Strain, discarding the skin and bone. Pour the liquid into a clean pan.

4 Add the milk, flaked fish and seasoning to the pan, bring to the boil and simmer for about 3 minutes.

5 Gradually whisk in sufficient mashed potato to give a fairly thick soup, then stir in the butter and sharpen to taste with lemon juice.

6 Add the fromage frais and 3 tablespoons of the chopped parsley. Reheat gently and adjust the seasoning. Sprinkle with the remaining parsley and serve immediately.

COOK'S TIP

Undyed smoked haddock may be used in place of the bright yellow fish; it will give a paler colour but just as much flavour. Alternatively, use smoked cod or smoked whiting.

Louisiana Seafood Gumbo

Gumbo is a hearty, thick soup, almost a stew. This New Orleans classic must be served with a scoop of hot, fluffy, cooked rice.

NUTRITIONAL INFORMATION

Calories . . . . . . .267 Sugars 6g
Protein . . . . .27g Fat 8g
Carbohydrate . . .24g Saturates 1g

5 MINS   35 MINS

SERVES 4

I N G R E D I E N T S

1 tbsp plain flour

1 tsp paprika

350 g/12 oz monkfish fillets, cut into chunks

2 tbsp olive oil

1 onion, chopped

1 green (bell) pepper, cored, seeded and chopped

3 celery sticks, finely chopped

2 garlic cloves, crushed

175 g/6 oz okra, sliced

600 ml/1 pint/2½ cups vegetable stock

1 x 425 g/15 oz can chopped tomatoes

1 bouquet garni

125 g/4½ oz peeled prawns (shrimp)

juice of 1 lemon

dash of Tabasco

2 tsp Worcestershire sauce

175 g/6 oz/generous 1 cup cooked long-grain American rice

1 Mix the flour with the paprika. Add the monkfish chunks and toss to coat well.

2 Heat the olive oil in a large, heavy-based pan. Add the monkfish pieces and fry until browned on all sides. Remove from the pan with a slotted spoon and set aside.

3 Add the onion, green (bell) pepper, celery, garlic and okra and fry gently for 5 minutes until softened.

4 Add the stock, tomatoes and bouquet garni. Bring to the boil, reduce the heat and simmer for 15 minutes.

5 Return the monkfish to the pan with the prawns (shrimp), lemon juice, Tabasco and Worcestershire sauces. Simmer for a further 5 minutes.

6 To serve, place a mound of cooked rice in each warmed, serving bowl, then ladle over the seafood gumbo.

Crab & Ginger Soup

Two classic ingredients in Chinese cooking are blended together in this recipe for a special soup.

NUTRITIONAL INFORMATION

Calories 32	Sugars 1g	
Protein 6g	Fat 0.4g	
Carbohydrate 1g	Saturates 0g	

 10 MINS   25 MINS

SERVES 4

I N G R E D I E N T S

1 carrot

1 leek

1 bay leaf

850 ml/1½ pints/3¾ cups fish stock

2 medium-sized cooked crabs

2.5-cm/1-inch piece fresh root ginger (ginger root), grated

1 tsp light soy sauce

½ tsp ground star anise

salt and pepper

1 Using a sharp knife, chop the carrot and leek into small pieces and place in a large saucepan with the bay leaf and fish stock.

2 Bring the mixture in the saucepan to the boil.

3 Reduce the heat, cover and leave to simmer for about 10 minutes, or until the vegetables are nearly tender.

4 Remove all of the meat from the cooked crabs. Break off and reserve the claws, break the joints and remove the meat, using a fork or skewer.

5 Add the crabmeat to the pan of fish stock, together with the ginger, soy sauce and star anise and bring to the boil. Leave to simmer for about 10 minutes, or until the vegetables are tender and the crab is heated through.

6 Season the soup then ladle into a warmed soup tureen or individual serving bowls and garnish with crab claws. Serve immediately.

VARIATION

If fresh crabmeat is unavailable, use drained canned crabmeat or thawed frozen crabmeat instead.

Mussel & Potato Soup

This quick and easy soup would make a delicious summer lunch, served with fresh crusty bread.

NUTRITIONAL INFORMATION

Calories 804	Sugars 3g	
Protein 17g	Fat 68g	
Carbohydrate ...32g	Saturates 38g	

 10 MINS   35 MINS

SERVES 4

INGREDIENTS

750 g/1 lb 10 oz mussels

2 tbsp olive oil

100 g/3½ oz/7 tbsp unsalted butter

2 slices rindless fatty bacon, chopped

1 onion, chopped

2 garlic cloves, crushed

60 g/2 oz/½ cup plain (all-purpose) flour

450 g/1 lb potatoes, thinly sliced

100 g/3½ oz/¾ cup dried conchigliette

300 ml/½ pint/1¼ cups double (heavy)
    cream

1 tbsp lemon juice

2 egg yolks

salt and pepper

TO GARNISH

2 tbsp finely chopped fresh parsley

lemon wedges

1 Debeard the mussels and scrub them under cold water for 5 minutes. Discard any mussels that do not close immediately when sharply tapped.

2 Bring a large pan of water to the boil, add the mussels, oil and a little pepper. Cook until the mussels open (discard any mussels that remain closed).

3 Drain the mussels, reserving the cooking liquid. Remove the mussels from their shells.

4 Melt the butter in a large saucepan, add the bacon, onion and garlic and cook for 4 minutes. Carefully stir in the flour. Measure 1.2 litres/2 pints/5 cups of the reserved cooking liquid and stir it into the pan.

5 Add the potatoes to the pan and simmer for 5 minutes. Add the conchigliette and simmer for a further 10 minutes.

6 Add the cream and lemon juice, season to taste with salt and pepper, then add the mussels to the pan.

7 Blend the egg yolks with 1-2 tbsp of the remaining cooking liquid, stir into the pan and cook for 4 minutes.

8 Ladle the soup into 4 warm individual soup bowls, garnish with the chopped fresh parsley and lemon wedges and serve immediately.

Potato & Mixed Fish Soup

Any mixture of fish is suitable for this recipe, from simple smoked and white fish to salmon or mussels, depending on the occasion.

NUTRITIONAL INFORMATION

Calories 458	Sugar 5g
Protein 28g	Fats 25g
Carbohydrates ...22g	Saturates 12g

10 MINS   35 MINS

SERVES 4

I N G R E D I E N T S

2 tbsp vegetable oil

450 g/1 lb small new potatoes, halved

1 bunch spring onions (scallions), sliced

1 yellow (bell) pepper, sliced

2 garlic cloves, crushed

225 ml/8 fl oz/1 cup dry white wine

600 ml/1 pint/2½ cups fish stock

225 g/8 oz white fish fillet, skinned and cubed

225 g/8 oz smoked cod fillet, skinned and cubed

2 tomatoes, peeled, seeded and chopped

100 g/3½ oz peeled cooked prawns (shrimp)

150 ml/¼ pint/⅔ cup double (heavy) cream

2 tbsp shredded fresh basil

1 Heat the vegetable oil in a large saucepan and add the halved potatoes, sliced spring onions (scallions) and (bell) pepper and the garlic. Sauté gently for 3 minutes, stirring constantly.

2 Add the white wine and fish stock to the saucepan and bring to the boil. Reduce the heat and simmer for 10-15 minutes.

3 Add the cubed fish fillets and the tomatoes to the soup and continue to cook for 10 minutes or until the fish is cooked through.

4 Stir in the prawns (shrimp), cream and shredded basil and cook for 2-3 minutes. Pour the soup into warmed bowls and serve immediately.

COOK'S TIP

For a soup which is slightly less rich, omit the wine and stir natural yogurt into the soup instead of the double (heavy) cream.

Salmon Bisque

A filling soup which is ideal for all types of occasion, from an elegant dinner to a picnic. For a touch of luxury, garnish with smoked salmon.

NUTRITIONAL INFORMATION

Calories	272	Sugars	.........1g
Protein	........17g	Fat	..........19g
Carbohydrate	....5g	Saturates	......8g

5 MINS   40 MINS

SERVES 4–6

INGREDIENTS

1–2 salmon heads (depending on size) or a tail piece of salmon weighing about 500 g/1 lb 2 oz

900 ml/1½ pints/3½ cups water

1 fresh or dried bay leaf

1 lemon, sliced

a few black peppercorns

30 g/1 oz/2 tbsp butter or margarine

2 tbsp finely chopped onion or spring onions (scallions)

30 g/1 oz/¼ cup plain (all-purpose) flour

150 ml/¼ pint /⅔ cup dry white wine or fish stock

150 ml/¼ pint/⅔ cup single (light) cream

1 tbsp chopped fresh fennel or dill

2–3 tsp lemon or lime juice

salt and pepper

TO GARNISH

30–45 g/1–1½ oz smoked salmon pieces, chopped (optional)

sprigs of fresh fennel or dill

1 Put the salmon, water, bay leaf, lemon and peppercorns into a saucepan. Bring to the boil, remove any scum from the surface, then cover the pan and simmer gently for 20 minutes until the fish is cooked through.

2 Remove from the heat, strain the stock and reserve 600 ml/1 pint/2½ cups. Remove and discard all the skin and bones from the salmon and flake the flesh, removing all the pieces from the head, if using.

3 Melt the butter or margarine in a saucepan and fry the onion or spring onions (scallions) gently for about 5 minutes until soft. Stir in the flour and cook for 1 minute then stir in the reserved stock and wine or fish stock. Bring to the boil, stirring. Add the salmon, season well, then simmer gently for about 5 minutes.

4 Add the cream and the chopped fennel or dill and reheat gently, but do not boil. Sharpen to taste with lemon or lime juice and season again. Serve hot or chilled, garnished with smoked salmon (if using) and sprigs of fennel or dill.

Italian Seafood Soup

This colourful mixed seafood soup would be superbly complemented by a dry white wine.

NUTRITIONAL INFORMATION

Calories 668	Sugars 3g
Protein 48g	Fat 43g
Carbohydrate ...21g	Saturates 25g

5 MINS   55 MINS

SERVES 4

INGREDIENTS

60 g/2 oz/4 tbsp butter

450 g/1 lb assorted fish fillets, such as red
   mullet and snapper

450 g/1 lb prepared seafood, such as squid
   and prawns (shrimp)

225 g/8 oz fresh crabmeat

1 large onion, sliced

25 g/1 oz/¼ cup plain (all-purpose) flour

1.2 litres/2 pints/5 cups fish stock

100 g/3 ½ oz/¾ cup dried pasta shapes,
   such as ditalini or elbow macaroni

1 tbsp anchovy essence (extract)

grated rind and juice of 1 orange

50 ml/2 fl oz/¼ cup dry sherry

300 ml/ ½ pint/1 ¼ cups double (heavy)
   cream

salt and pepper

crusty brown bread, to serve

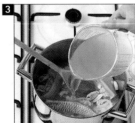
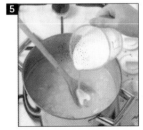

1 Melt the butter in a large saucepan, add the fish fillets, seafood, crabmeat and onion and cook gently over a low heat for 6 minutes.

2 Add the flour to the seafood mixture, stirring thoroughly to avoid any lumps from forming.

3 Gradually add the stock, stirring, until the soup comes to the boil. Reduce the heat and simmer for 30 minutes.

4 Add the pasta to the pan and cook for a further 10 minutes.

5 Stir in the anchovy essence, orange rind, orange juice, sherry and double (heavy) cream. Season to taste with salt and pepper.

6 Heat the soup until completely warmed through.

7 Transfer the soup to a tureen or to warm soup bowls and serve with crusty brown bread.

Prawn (Shrimp) Gumbo

This soup is thick with onions, red (bell) peppers, rice, prawns (shrimp) and okra, which both adds flavour and acts as a thickening agent.

NUTRITIONAL INFORMATION

Calories 177   Sugar 5g
Protein . . . . .12g   Fats 8g
Carbohydrates . . .15g   Saturates 1g

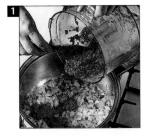
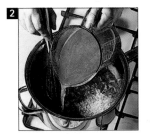

1 HOUR   45 MINS

SERVES 4–6

INGREDIENTS

1 large onion, chopped finely

2 slices lean bacon, chopped finely (optional)

1–2 garlic cloves, crushed

2 tbsp olive oil

1 large or 2 small red (bell) peppers, chopped finely or minced coarsely

850 ml/1½ pints/3½ cups fish or vegetable stock

1 fresh or dried bay leaf

1 blade mace

good pinch of ground allspice

40 g/1½ oz/3 tbsp long-grain rice

1 tbsp white wine vinegar

125–175 g/4½–6 oz okra, trimmed and sliced very thinly

90–125 g/3–4½ oz/½–⅔ cup peeled prawns (shrimp)

1 tbsp anchovy essence (paste)

2 tsp tomato purée (paste)

1–2 tbsp chopped fresh parsley

salt and pepper

TO GARNISH

whole prawns (shrimp)

sprigs of fresh parsley

1 Gently fry the onion, bacon (if using) and garlic in the oil in a large saucepan for 4–5 minutes until soft. Add the (bell) peppers to the pan and continue to fry gently for a couple of minutes.

2 Add the stock, bay leaf, mace, allspice, rice, vinegar and seasoning and bring to the boil. Cover and simmer gently for about 20 minutes, giving an occasional stir, until the rice is just tender.

3 Add the okra, prawns (shrimp), anchovy essence (paste) and tomato purée (paste), cover and simmer gently for about 15 minutes until the okra is tender and the mixture slightly thickened.

4 Discard the bay leaf and mace from the soup and adjust the seasoning. Stir in the parsley and serve each portion garnished with a whole prawn (shrimp) and parsley sprigs.

Partan Bree

This traditional Scottish soup is thickened with a purée of rice and crab meat cooked in milk. Add soured cream, if liked, at the end of cooking.

NUTRITIONAL INFORMATION

Calories 112   Sugars 5g
Protein . . . . .7g   Fat 2g
Carbohydrate . . .18g   Saturates 0.3g

1 HOUR   35 MINS

SERVES 6

INGREDIENTS

1 medium-sized boiled crab

90 g/3 oz/scant ½ cup long-grain rice

600 ml/1 pint/2½ cups skimmed milk

600 ml/1 pint/2½ cups fish stock

1 tbsp anchovy essence (paste)

2 tsp lime or lemon juice

1 tbsp chopped fresh parsley or I tsp
   chopped fresh thyme

3–4 tbsp soured cream (optional)

salt and pepper

snipped chives, to garnish

1 Remove and reserve all the brown and white meat from the crab, then crack the claws and remove and chop that meat; reserve the claw meat.

COOK'S TIP

If you are unable to buy a whole crab, use about 175 g/6 oz frozen crab meat and thaw thoroughly before use; or a 175 g/6 oz can of crab meat which just needs thorough draining.

2 Put the rice and milk into a saucepan and bring slowly to the boil. Cover and simmer gently for about 20 minutes.

3 Add the reserved white and brown crab meat and seasoning and simmer for a further 5 minutes.

4 Cool a little, then press through a sieve (strainer), or blend in a food processor or blender until smooth.

5 Pour the soup into a clean saucepan and add the fish stock and the reserved claw meat. Bring slowly to the boil, then add the anchovy essence (paste) and lime or lemon juice and adjust the seasoning.

6 Simmer for a further 2–3 minutes. Stir in the parsley or thyme and then swirl soured cream (if using) through each serving. Garnish with snipped chives.

Minestrone & Pasta Soup

Italian cooks have created some very heart-warming soups and this is the most famous of all.

NUTRITIONAL INFORMATION

Calories 231	Sugars 3g	
Protein 8g	Fat 16g	
Carbohydrate . . .14g	Saturates 7g	

10 MINS   1¾ HOURS

SERVES 10

I N G R E D I E N T S

3 garlic cloves

3 large onions

2 celery sticks (sticks)

2 large carrots

2 large potatoes

100 g/3½ oz French (green) beans

100 g/3½ oz courgettes (zucchini)

60 g/2 oz/4 tbsp butter

50 ml/2 fl oz/¼ cup olive oil

60 g/2 oz rindless fatty bacon, finely diced

1.5 litres/2¾ pints/6⅞ cups vegetable or
  chicken stock

1 bunch fresh basil, finely chopped

100 g/3½ oz chopped tomatoes

2 tbsp tomato purée (paste)

100 g/3½ oz Parmesan cheese rind

90 g/3 oz dried spaghetti, broken up

salt and pepper

freshly grated Parmesan cheese, to serve

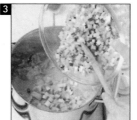

1 Finely chop the garlic, onions, celery, carrots, potatoes, beans and courgettes (zucchini).

2 Heat the butter and oil together in a large saucepan, add the bacon and cook for 2 minutes.

3 Add the garlic and onion and fry for 2 minutes, then stir in the celery, carrots and potatoes and fry for a further 2 minutes.

4 Add the beans to the pan and fry for 2 minutes. Stir in the courgettes (zucchini) and fry for a further 2 minutes. Cover the pan and cook all the vegetables, stirring frequently, for 15 minutes.

5 Add the stock, basil, tomatoes, tomato purée (paste) and cheese rind and season to taste. Bring to the boil, lower the heat and simmer for 1 hour. Remove and discard the cheese rind.

6 Add the spaghetti to the pan and cook for 20 minutes. Serve in large, warm soup bowls; sprinkle with freshly grated Parmesan cheese.

Bean & Pasta Soup

A dish with proud Mediterranean origins, this soup is a winter warmer.
Serve with warm, crusty bread and, if you like, a slice of cheese.

NUTRITIONAL INFORMATION

Calories	463	Sugars	.........5g
Protein	........13g	Fat	..........33g
Carbohydrate	...30g	Saturates	.......7g

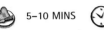 5–10 MINS   1¼ HOURS

SERVES 4

INGREDIENTS

225 g/8 oz/generous 1 cup dried haricot
   (navy) beans, soaked, drained and rinsed

4 tbsp olive oil

2 large onions, sliced

3 garlic cloves, chopped

400 g/14 oz can chopped tomatoes

1 tsp dried oregano

1 tsp tomato purée (paste)

850 ml/1 ½ pints/3 ½ cups water

90 g/3 oz small pasta shapes, such as fusilli
   or conchigliette

125 g/4 ½ oz sun-dried tomatoes, drained
   and sliced thinly

1 tbsp chopped coriander (cilantro),
   or flat-leaf parsley

2 tbsp freshly grated Parmesan

salt and pepper

1 Put the soaked beans into a large pan,
cover with cold water and bring them
to the boil. Boil rapidly for 15 minutes to
remove any harmful toxins. Drain the
beans in a colander.

2 Heat the oil in a pan over a medium
heat and fry the onions until they are
just beginning to change colour. Stir in the
garlic and cook for 1 further minute. Stir
in the chopped tomatoes, oregano and the
tomato purée (paste) and pour on the
water. Add the beans, bring to the boil and
cover the pan. Simmer for 45 minutes or
until the beans are almost tender.

3 Add the pasta, season the soup with
salt and pepper to taste and stir in the
sun-dried tomatoes. Return the soup to
the boil, partly cover the pan and continue
cooking for 10 minutes, or until the pasta
is nearly tender.

4 Stir in the chopped coriander
(cilantro) or parsley. Taste the soup
and adjust the seasoning if necessary.
Transfer to a warmed soup tureen to serve.
Sprinkle with the cheese and serve hot.

Indian Bean Soup

A thick and hearty soup, nourishing and substantial enough to serve as a main meal with wholemeal (whole wheat) bread.

NUTRITIONAL INFORMATION

Calories 237	Sugars 9g	
Protein 9g	Fat 9g	
Carbohydrate ...33g	Saturates 1g	

 20 MINS   50 MINS

SERVES 6

I N G R E D I E N T S

4 tbsp vegetable ghee or vegetable oil

2 onions, peeled and chopped

225 g/8 oz/1½ cups potato, cut
into chunks

225 g/8 oz/1½ cups parsnip, cut
into chunks

225 g/8 oz/1½ cups turnip or swede
(rutabaga), cut into chunks

2 celery sticks, sliced

2 courgettes (zucchini), sliced

1 green (bell) pepper, seeded and cut into
1 cm/½ inch pieces

2 garlic cloves, crushed

2 tsp ground coriander

1 tbsp paprika

1 tbsp mild curry paste

1.2 litres/2 pints/5 cups vegetable stock

salt

400 g/14 oz can black-eye beans (peas),
drained and rinsed

chopped coriander (cilantro),
to garnish (optional)

1 Heat the ghee or oil in a saucepan, add all the prepared vegetables, except the courgettes (zucchini) and green (bell) pepper, and cook over a moderate heat, stirring frequently, for 5 minutes. Add the garlic, ground coriander, paprika and curry paste and cook, stirring constantly, for 1 minute.

2 Stir in the stock and season with salt to taste. Bring to the boil, cover and simmer over a low heat, stirring occasionally, for 25 minutes.

3 Stir in the black-eye beans (peas), sliced courgettes (zucchini) and green (bell) pepper, cover and continue cooking for a further 15 minutes, or until all the vegetables are tender.

4 Process 300 ml/½ pint/1¼ cups of the soup mixture (about 2 ladlefuls) in a food processor or blender. Return the puréed mixture to the soup in the saucepan and reheat until piping hot. Sprinkle with chopped coriander (cilantro), if using and serve hot.

Brown Lentil & Pasta Soup

In Italy, this soup is called *Minestrade Lentiche*. A *minestra* is a soup cooked with pasta; here, farfalline, a small bow-shaped variety, is used.

NUTRITIONAL INFORMATION

Calories 225	Sugars 1g
Protein 13g	Fat 8g
Carbohydrate ...27g	Saturates 3g

 5 MINS   25 MINS

SERVES 4

INGREDIENTS

4 rashers streaky bacon, cut into small
   squares

1 onion, chopped

2 garlic cloves, crushed

2 sticks celery, chopped

50 g/1 ¾ oz/ ¼ cup farfalline or spaghetti,
   broken into small pieces

1 x 400 g/14 oz can brown lentils, drained

1.2 litres/2 pints/5 cups hot ham or
   vegetable stock

2 tbsp chopped, fresh mint

1 Place the bacon in a large frying pan (skillet) together with the onions, garlic and celery. Dry fry for 4–5 minutes, stirring, until the onion is tender and the bacon is just beginning to brown.

2 Add the pasta to the pan (skillet) and cook, stirring, for about 1 minute to coat the pasta in the oil.

3 Add the lentils and the stock and bring to the boil. Reduce the heat and leave to simmer for 12–15 minutes or until the pasta is tender.

4 Remove the pan (skillet) from the heat and stir in the chopped fresh mint.

5 Transfer the soup to warm soup bowls and serve immediately.

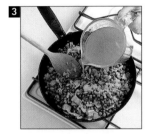

COOK'S TIP

If you prefer to use dried lentils, add the stock before the pasta and cook for 1–1¼ hours until the lentils are tender. Add the pasta and cook for a further 12–15 minutes.

Tuscan Bean Soup

This thick, satisfying blend of beans and diced vegetables in a rich red wine and tomato stock makes an ideal simple supper dish.

NUTRITIONAL INFORMATION

Calories 164   Sugars 10g
Protein ....9g   Fat 1g
Carbohydrate ...26g   Saturates 0g

1 HOUR   30 MINS

SERVES 4

I N G R E D I E N T S

1 medium onion, chopped

1 garlic clove, finely chopped

2 celery sticks, sliced

1 large carrot, diced

400 g/14 oz can chopped tomatoes

150 ml/5 fl oz/⅔ cup Italian dry red wine

1.2 litres/2 pints/5 cups fresh vegetable stock

1 tsp dried oregano

425 g/15 oz can mixed beans and pulses

2 medium courgettes (zucchini), diced

1 tbsp tomato purée (paste)

salt and pepper

TO SERVE

low-fat pesto sauce

crusty bread

1 Place the prepared onion, garlic, celery and carrot in a large saucepan. Stir in the tomatoes, red wine, vegetable stock and oregano.

2 Bring the vegetable mixture to the boil, cover and simmer for 15 minutes.

3 Stir the mixed beans and pulses, and courgettes (zucchini) into the mixture in the saucepan, and continue to cook, uncovered, for 5 minutes.

4 Add the tomato purée (paste) to the mixture and season well with salt and pepper to taste. Heat through gently, stirring occasionally, for a further 2–3 minutes.

5 Ladle the soup into warm bowls and serve with a spoonful of low-fat pesto on each portion and accompanied with crusty bread. Serve immediately.

COOK'S TIP

For a more substantial soup, add 350 g/12 oz diced lean cooked chicken or turkey with the tomato purée (paste) in step 4.

Spicy Dhal & Carrot Soup

This nutritious soup uses split red lentils and carrots as the two main ingredients and includes a selection of spices to give it a kick.

NUTRITIONAL INFORMATION

Calories . . . . . . .173 Sugars 11g
Protein . . . . .9g Fat 5g
Carbohydrate . . .24g Saturates 1g

15 MINS 45 MINS

SERVES 6

I N G R E D I E N T S

125 g/4½ oz split red lentils

1.2 litres/2 pints/5 cups vegetable stock

350 g/12 oz carrots, sliced

2 onions, chopped

225 g/8 oz can chopped tomatoes

2 garlic cloves, chopped

2 tbsp vegetable ghee or oil

1 tsp ground cumin

1 tsp ground coriander

1 fresh green chilli, seeded and chopped,
   or 1 tsp minced chilli

½ tsp ground turmeric

1 tbsp lemon juice

salt

300 ml/½ pint/1¼ cups milk

2 tbsp chopped coriander (cilantro)

natural (unsweetened) yogurt, to serve

1 Place the lentils in a strainer and rinse well under cold running water. Drain and place in a large saucepan, together with 850 ml/1½ pints/3½ cups of the stock, the carrots, onions, tomatoes and garlic. Bring the mixture to the boil, reduce the heat, cover and simmer for 30 minutes or until the vegetables and lentils are tender.

2 Meanwhile, heat the ghee or oil in a small pan. Add the cumin, ground coriander, chilli and turmeric and fry over a low heat for 1 minute. Remove from the heat and stir in the lemon juice. Season with salt to taste.

3 Process the soup in batches in a blender or food processor. Return the

soup to the saucepan, add the spice mixture and the remaining 300 ml/ ½ pint/1¼ cups stock and simmer over a low heat for 10 minutes.

4 Add the milk, taste and adjust the seasoning, if necessary. Stir in the chopped coriander (cilantro) and reheat gently. Serve hot with a swirl of yogurt.

Mixed Bean Soup

This is a really hearty soup, filled with colour, flavour and goodness, which may be adapted to any vegetables that you have at hand.

NUTRITIONAL INFORMATION

Calories 190	Sugars 9g	
Protein 10g	Fat 4g	
Carbohydrate ...30g	Saturates 0.5g	

 10 MINS   40 MINS

SERVES 4

INGREDIENTS

1 tbsp vegetable oil

1 red onion, halved and sliced

100 g/3½ oz/⅔ cup potato, diced

1 carrot, diced

1 leek, sliced

1 green chilli, sliced

3 garlic cloves, crushed

1 tsp ground coriander

1 tsp chilli powder

1 litre/1¾ pints/4 cups vegetable stock

450 g/1 lb mixed canned beans,
   such as red kidney, borlotti, black eye
   or flageolet, drained

salt and pepper

2 tbsp chopped coriander (cilantro),
   to garnish

1 Heat the vegetable oil in a large saucepan. Add the onion, potato, carrot and leek and sauté, stirring constantly, for about 2 minutes, until the vegetables are slightly softened.

2 Add the sliced chilli and crushed garlic and cook for a further 1 minute.

3 Stir in the ground coriander, chilli powder and the vegetable stock.

4 Bring the soup to the boil, reduce the heat and cook for 20 minutes, or until the vegetables are tender.

5 Stir in the beans, season well with salt and pepper and cook, stirring occasionally, for a further 10 minutes.

6 Transfer the soup to a warm tureen or individual bowls, garnish with chopped coriander (cilantro) and serve.

COOK'S TIP

Serve this soup with slices of warm corn bread or a cheese loaf.

Minestrone Soup

Minestrone translates as 'big soup' in Italian. It is made all over Italy, but this version comes from Livorno, a port on the western coast.

NUTRITIONAL INFORMATION

Calories 311	Sugars 8g
Protein 12g	Fat 19g
Carbohydrate . . .26g	Saturates 5g

 10 MINS   30 MINS

SERVES 4

I N G R E D I E N T S

1 tbsp olive oil

100 g/3½ oz pancetta ham, diced

2 medium onions, chopped

2 cloves garlic, crushed

1 potato, peeled and cut into 1 cm/
½ inch cubes

1 carrot, peeled and cut into chunks

1 leek, sliced into rings

¼ green cabbage, shredded

1 stick celery, chopped

450 g/1 lb can chopped tomatoes

200 g/7 oz can flageolet (small navy)
beans, drained and rinsed

600 ml/1 pint/2½ cups hot ham or chicken
stock, diluted with 600 ml/1 pint/2½ cups
boiling water

bouquet garni (2 bay leaves, 2 sprigs
rosemary and 2 sprigs thyme, tied
together)

salt and pepper

freshly grated Parmesan cheese, to serve

1 Heat the olive oil in a large saucepan. Add the diced pancetta, chopped onions and garlic and fry for about 5 minutes, stirring, or until the onions are soft and golden.

2 Add the prepared potato, carrot, leek, cabbage and celery to the saucepan. Cook for a further 2 minutes, stirring frequently, to coat all of the vegetables in the oil.

3 Add the tomatoes, flageolet (small navy) beans, hot ham or chicken stock and bouquet garni to the pan, stirring to mix. Leave the soup to simmer, covered, for 15–20 minutes or until all of the vegetables are just tender.

4 Remove the bouquet garni, season with salt and pepper to taste and serve with plenty of freshly grated Parmesan cheese.

Creamy Tuscan Bean Soup

A thick and creamy soup that is based on a traditional Tuscan recipe. If you use dried beans, the preparation and cooking times will be longer.

NUTRITIONAL INFORMATION

Calories	250	Sugars	........4g
Protein	........13g	Fat	..........10g
Carbohydrate	...29g	Saturates	.......2g

🍲 2 MINS   🕐 10 MINS

SERVES 4

I N G R E D I E N T S

225 g/8 oz dried butter beans, soaked
   overnight, or 2 x 400 g/14 oz can butter
   beans

1 tbsp olive oil

2 garlic cloves, crushed

1 vegetable or chicken stock cube,
   crumbled

150 ml/¼ pint/⅔ cup milk

2 tbsp chopped fresh oregano

salt and pepper

1 If you are using dried beans that have been soaked overnight, drain them thoroughly. Bring a large pan of water to the boil, add the beans and boil for 10 minutes. Cover the pan and simmer for a further 30 minutes or until tender. Drain the beans, reserving the cooking liquid. If you are using canned beans, drain them thoroughly and reserve the liquid.

2 Heat the oil in a large frying pan (skillet) and fry the garlic for 2–3 minutes or until just beginning to brown.

3 Add the beans and 400 ml/14 fl oz/1⅔ cup of the reserved liquid to the pan (skillet), stirring. You may need to add a little water if there is insufficient liquid. Stir in the crumbled stock cube. Bring the mixture to the boil and then remove the pan from the heat.

4 Place the bean mixture in a food processor and blend to form a smooth purée. Alternatively, mash the bean mixture to a smooth consistency. Season to taste with salt and pepper and stir in the milk.

5 Pour the soup back into the pan and gently heat to just below boiling point. Stir in the chopped oregano just before serving.

Dhal Soup

Dhal is the name given to a delicious Indian lentil dish. This soup is a variation of the theme – it is made with red lentils and curry powder.

NUTRITIONAL INFORMATION

Calories	284	Sugars	........13g
Protein	........16g	Fat	..........9g
Carbohydrate	...38g	Saturates	.......5g

 5 MINS   40 MINS

SERVES 4

I N G R E D I E N T S

25 g/1 oz/2 tbsp butter

2 garlic cloves, crushed

1 onion, chopped

½ tsp turmeric

1 tsp garam masala

¼ tsp chilli powder

1 tsp ground cumin

1 kg/2 lb 4 oz canned, chopped
    tomatoes, drained

175 g/6 oz/1 cup red lentils

2 tsp lemon juice

600 ml/1 pint/2½ cups vegetable stock

300 ml/½ pint/1¼ cups coconut milk

salt and pepper

chopped coriander (cilantro) and lemon
    slices, to garnish

naan bread, to serve

1 Melt the butter in a large saucepan. Add the garlic and onion and sauté, stirring, for 2–3 minutes. Add the turmeric, garam masala, chilli powder and cumin and cook for a further 30 seconds.

2 Stir in the tomatoes, red lentils, lemon juice, vegetable stock and coconut milk and bring to the boil.

3 Reduce the heat to low and simmer the soup, uncovered, for about 25–30 minutes, until the lentils are tender and cooked.

4 Season to taste with salt and pepper and ladle the soup into a warm tureen. Garnish with chopped coriander (cilantro) and lemon slices and serve immediately with warm naan bread.

COOK'S TIP

You can buy cans of coconut milk from supermarkets and delicatessens. It can also be made by grating creamed coconut, which comes in the form of a solid bar, and then mixing it with water.

Lentil & Parsnip Pottage

Smooth and delicious, this soup has the most glorious golden colour and a fabulous flavour.

NUTRITIONAL INFORMATION

Calories	82	Sugars	. . . . .4g
Protein	. . . . .6g	Fat	. . . . .1g
Carbohydrate	. . .13g	Saturates	. . . . .0.3g

 5 MINS   55 MINS

SERVES 4

INGREDIENTS

3 slices lean streaky bacon, chopped

1 onion, chopped

2 carrots, chopped

2 parsnips, chopped

60 g/2 oz/⅓ cup red lentils

1 litre/1¾ pints/4 cups vegetable stock or water

salt and pepper

chopped fresh chives to garnish

1 Heat a large saucepan, add the bacon and dry-fry for 5 minutes until crisp and golden.

2 Add the onion, carrots and parsnips and cook for about 5 minutes without browning.

3 Add the lentils to the saucepan and stir to mix with the vegetables.

4 Add the stock or water to the pan and bring to the boil. Cover and simmer for 30–40 minutes until tender.

5 Transfer the soup to a blender or food processor and blend for about 15 seconds until smooth. Alternatively, press the soup through a sieve (strainer).

6 Return to the saucepan and reheat gently until almost boiling.

7 Season the soup with salt and pepper to taste.

8 Garnish the lentil and parsnip pottage with chopped fresh chives and serve at once.

COOK'S TIP

For a meatier soup, use a knuckle of ham in place of the streaky bacon. Cook it for $1^1/_2$–2 hours before adding the vegetables and lentils and use the ham's cooking liquid as the stock.

This is a Parragon Book
This edition published in 2001

Parragon
Queen Street House
4 Queen Street
Bath BA1 1HE, UK

ISBN 0-75256-162-6

Printed in Italy

With grateful thanks to Claire Dashwood.

Material in this book has previously appeared in Ultimate Recipes Low Fat, Ultimate Recipes Vegetarian, Ultimate Recipes Italian, Ultimate Recipes Chinese, originally produced by Haldane Mason, London.

Notes
Use all metric or all imperial quantities, as the two are not interchangeable. Cup measurements in this book are for American cups. Tablespoons are assumed to be 15 ml. Unless otherwise stated, milk is assumed to be full fat, eggs are medium and pepper is freshly ground black pepper.

The nutritional information provided for each recipe is per serving or per portion. Optional ingredients, variations or serving suggestions have not been included in the calculations. The times given for each recipe are an approximate guide only as the preparation times may differ as a result of the type of oven used.